5 STEPS
TO FREEDOM

5 STEPS TO FREEDOM

How to Cut Your Dependence on Institutions and Escape Financial Slavery

By

JEFF NABERS

and

PHOEBE CHONGCHUA

5 Steps to Freedom: How to Cut Your Dependence on Institutions and Escape Financial Slavery / Jeff Nabers, Phoebe Chongchua

ISBN-10: 0-9824313-0-9
ISBN-13: 987-0-9824313-0-6

Cover design by Anton Heil

TABLE OF CONTENTS

PREFACE

We have just seen the largest financial failures and collapses in our nation's short history. If you are like most Americans, you're at a loss for ideas. You want to believe the rosy predictions from the very "experts" whose last rosy predictions led us right into this situation. We all want to believe that things will just get better somehow all on their own.

And we're being told exactly what we want to hear, just like when a woman asks her husband, "Does this dress make me look fat?" Contrary to the reality of our economy looking enormously fat in this dress, the experts are soothing our concerns.

"The worst is behind us."

Unlike in the husband-wife scenario, being told what we want to hear will lead to dire circumstances. If watching the stock market lose 40 percent of its price in 2008 upset you, then continuing to subscribe to popular opinion is going to go beyond upsetting you—it's going to break you.

Perhaps the most disappointing part of what lies ahead on the popular path is that you are being prepped for the ultimate deception. Only this will be different than watching a woman be sawn in two on a magician's stage. Instead of seeing something horrific that isn't real, you will see something that appears to be perfectly fine, while the horrific truth lies beneath the surface.

If you do nothing, the illusions woven into your life will lead you to work harder and longer for less, and you won't even notice your slavery until it's too late. But that's if you do nothing. *This book is about taking action.*

But I'm not smart.

I'm not good with numbers.

Economics and investing are boring.

I'm really busy and don't have much free time.

Guess what? You don't need to have lots of free time, or be smart, good with numbers, interested in economics, or interested in investing to follow the 5 steps to freedom. The only requirement is that you must be prepared to unlearn.

Things aren't as complicated as many would have you believe. The lessons we will cover are a matter of unraveling confusing and downright incorrect ideas and replacing them with the plain and simple truth.

If you graduated from high school you have 14,000 hours worth of education encouraging the idea that you should:

1. Go to work to make money
2. Spend less than you earn
3. Save and/or invest the remainder of your earnings for your future

Item 3 of this prescribed life plan is where conventional wisdom broke down at a particular moment in 1971 and has never recovered since.

I won't debate the merits of working for money, or spending less than you earn. I also won't argue against saving or investing. But I will prove to you that what common knowledge considers saving and investing *isn't saving and investing at all.*

The popular version of saving and investing is a way of siphoning away your wealth and future, and you can put an end to that once and for all.

Your freedom awaits.

INTRODUCTION

CHAPTER ONE

THE LARGER FREEDOM

"They who can give up essential liberty to obtain a little temporary safety, deserve neither liberty nor safety."
- Benjamin Franklin

As America's troubles are snowballing, we're told to patiently allow the government to do whatever it takes to solve it all. Meanwhile, our individual rights to life, liberty, and the pursuit of happiness have taken a back seat to the selfish interests of politicians, officers of large corporations, and their friends.

What made this the greatest country in the world wasn't that we all *imagined* we were great. It was that we were a society of people free to pursue our own prosperity without interference from the government. The Constitution isn't perfect, but it represents the best foundation for government constructed thus far in human history. Unfortunately, the government itself violates the Constitution every minute of every day. One consequence is that our free market is less free nearly every time a new law is passed, and nearly every one of these new laws costs taxpayers money that we should rightfully be able to keep.

The Constitution grants so little authority to the federal government that it's only a 6-page document. All other governing, according to the U.S. Constitution, is the domain of the states. Yet the *United States Code* (federal laws) and the *Code of Federal Regulations* are over 50,000 pages each and growing. Not a single person on earth has read them in their entirety. That should give you an idea of how much our federal government is out of control.

Thus, the grounds for battle emerge.

A battle is being waged to restore our government to serve its limited and lawful purpose as defined by the Constitution, and many dedicated, respectable persons are leading the way. If you want the government to stop the tinkering that has provably caused or worsened virtually every recession and depression in the last 150 years, you owe it to yourself to join the movement to restore our country's greatness.

One benefit of the coming restoration could be the elimination of income taxes. If you think that sounds crazy, consider that removing the federal income tax today would only require our government to return to its spending levels of less than a decade ago. Most of the government benefits you enjoy (such as the police and fire departments) are provided by your local municipality, and not by the federal government. Not only is it possible to live in a country free of federal income taxes, many of the country's problems would be solved as a result. Entrepreneurs who stand to make a profit (or lose money and go out of business) do a better job of solving problems than a government that doesn't automatically go out of business when it does a poor job.

The ties between the government and banks, large corporations, and Wall Street powerhouses are strong, but the power they hold is power we have handed to them. The good news is that we can take that power away from them and stop the abuse. There are two angles of attack. One is to reform the government in an organized manner. The other is for each of us to take back our wealth into our own hands. The latter is built into the 5 steps to freedom presented herein, and it compliments and magnifies the former. Following the 5 steps contained in this book will not only liberate you as an individual, but it will have a direct impact on making the United States a free country again.

CHAPTER TWO

REPROGRAMMING BELIEFS

O n September 11, 2001, I was sleeping in when my phone woke me. It was my friend Justin.

"What are you doing?" he asked.

"I was sleeping until you woke me up," I replied.

"Well forget about whatever you were going to do today," said Justin.

"Why is that?"

"A plane just flew into the World Trade Center."

"What?"

"A plane just flew into the World Trade Center." Justin repeated.

"What do you mean? Why?" I envisioned a tiny two-passenger Cessna airplane bumping into a giant building, bouncing off, and leaving a little scrape that workers would repair within a few days. It seemed Justin woke me up to tell me about a bizarre accident.

"I don't know why the plane flew into the building. Just turn on the TV."

I pressed the power button on the TV while thinking that Justin should have waited until later in the day to tell me about the story.

"Which channel? What should I be looking for?" I asked groggily.

"Any channel. Seriously, any channel."

The actual events weren't registering. The TV lit up, and the footage of the big jet looped over and over. I was confused. At first, the reporters were no more certain about what was going on than I. Then the second plane hit the World Trade Center.

That's when it registered that this was a deliberate attack. I sat glued to the TV for hours. This was not akin to slowly rubbernecking past a car wreck on the highway. Car crashes are part of life. This was something different. It was hard to *comprehend*. It didn't fit into my understanding of the world. As far as I was concerned, the United States of America was the greatest country in the world. We had the best schools, the best jobs, the best homes, the best movies, the best food, the best everything. Why would anyone attack us?

This had never happened before, so it was outside my understanding of what *could* happen. The hours I spent glued to the TV that morning and afternoon reshaped my beliefs about what can happen to our country and in our world.

You may have had a similar experience when the financial meltdown tore through our economy in late 2008. At first, you probably didn't think it was that serious. Smart advisors and news reporters declared it a "hiccup" in the stock market. "Probably those damn mortgage brokers' fault," everyone thought. It was hard to comprehend. A huge failure of the entire U.S. financial system simply wasn't part of our picture of what could happen. We are the greatest country on earth. We have the brightest minds and the latest technology. Our financial system is the best out there. Banking failures and stock market collapses existed only in history books and small countries in Africa.

But, as you sat glued to the TV for weeks or months, you had no choice but to realize that our system was actually broken. We bailed out AIG with taxpayer dollars. One week later AIG threw a $440,000 party. Then we bailed out AIG again. The company promptly paid $165 million in executive bonuses. Then we bailed them out a third time. "Where's the punch line of this joke?" I asked my computer monitor as I read the news. No reply.

Or consider the failure of Washington Mutual Bank. The CEO of WaMu resigned as it was going under. A new CEO stepped in to work for the 17 days that it took for the government to arrange for JPMorgan Chase to take over WaMu. The 17-day CEO walked away with $19.1 million as a signing bonus and a cash severance package while shareholders lost millions. That's over $100,000 per hour for merely sitting on his hands while the government seized his bank!

Add to the mix the financial failure and/or bailout of countless other financial institutions that you learned about as you were glued to the TV for those weeks or months, and you probably began to swallow the truth: *Our financial system actually broke.*

This book sits in your hands right now because you know better than to believe this failed and broken financial system will honor its promises to you.

You need to prepare for what's around the corner. I have a cure for the economic bipolar disorder that leads you to be happy when things are going up and depressed when things are going down. Breaking through illusions will show you that the system which steals from you does so regardless of how much things are going up or down, and that the up and down movements just serve to distract you.

STEP 1: MEASURE

CHAPTER THREE

A NEW SCOREBOARD

What if every time you looked at a bank or portfolio statement you were being grossly misled? What you're about to grasp will be shocking, yet simple.

The dollar is an inconstant unit of measurement.

Read that over again. It's only an eight-word sentence, but letting those eight words sink in may be the most crucial step to escaping financial slavery.

That's right, the dollar isn't a concrete thing. We measure football fields in yards, yards in feet, and feet in inches—all constant units of measurement. Scoring a touchdown in football requires yards to be a constant unit of measurement. If you have a ruler and you mark two points on a piece of paper that are 6 inches apart, when you come back later, whether in 10 minutes or 10 years, you will find that the two marks are still 6 inches apart. That's because the ruler and its units of measurement stayed the same.

That's how dollars used to work too. The Constitution says that our money must be gold and silver. This is because the supply of gold and silver is somewhat constant, although not perfectly so. A constant money supply is absolutely required for money to serve its intended purpose.

Remember, money has no value in and of itself. It's not too useful to eat, wear, travel on, or live in. It just serves as a unit of exchange so that we don't have to deal with the harsh limitations of the barter system. Without money, if you grow corn and need clothes, you have to either find a clothes maker who needs corn or find a middleman who wants corn and has whatever the clothes maker wants. Money serves as the universal middleman, allowing any two parties to make an exchange. But this is all based on the idea of a constant money supply.

In 1971, the U.S. money supply became inconstant. Richard Nixon severed the link between our paper dollar and its gold backing. Since then, a privately owned banking organization known as the Federal Reserve has been free to manipulate our money supply. And in the 1970's, they started increasing it. This is like changing how long an inch is. When your ruler is slowly shifting in size, you'll find that 6 inches on the ruler no longer matches up with the two marks you made on the paper.

With money, think of it this way. If there were a total money supply of $1 million and you had $100,000, you would have 10 percent of the money. This gives you 10 percent of the buying power. Now, imagine that one day a banker decides to double the money supply without giving you any of the new money. That brings the total money supply to $2 million while you still have $100,000. You went from having 10 percent of the buying power to having only 5 percent of the buying power. This is inflation, but not the kind that financial experts talk about. Think of it as the money supply inflating.

That's a very simple example, and you have certainly never had 10 percent of the nation's buying power, but no matter the scale the fundamentals don't change. Theoretically, if new money is created and distributed to all proportionately, there is no real effect. In practice, when the money supply is increased, the new money is never distributed equally or to everyone.

The basic *effect* of inflation is price increases. One thing you must get straight is that inflation itself is not an increase in prices—it's an increase in the money supply.

In a free market inflation leads clearly and directly to increased prices. In a free market, the two are so directly connected that experts tell us that inflation *is* an increase in prices. That may not seem to matter, but it is a disastrous assertion. To think of inflation as an increase in prices focuses your attention on the *result* of money manipulation rather than the *cause*. This would be no problem in a free market, but we don't have a free market. We have a free*ish* market.

We may not live in a communist state, but we do have a growing number of constraints on the market. It is ridden with taxes, tariffs, free trade agreements (trading freely doesn't require an agreement), minimum wage laws, parity pricing, price fixing, subsidies, interest rate manipulation, forced bailouts, selective bailouts, and tens of thousands of pages of regulations enforced by regulators who don't follow their own regulations themselves.

So in this free*ish* market, increasing the money supply doesn't raise all prices equally and immediately. The price of one thing may go up while another goes down. The government may step in and interfere with one thing one way, interfere with another thing another way, and leave a third thing completely alone.

And we are all told to pay attention to prices. The money supply is rarely mentioned. In fact, the Fed (who single-handedly increases the money supply) *stopped reporting* its data about the money supply. For decades experts had talked up a storm about consumer prices in lieu of mentioning the money supply. Naturally, nothing was said when the Fed ceased publication of its M3 money supply reports in 2006.

Yet we know that inflation is something to be concerned about. That concern can't be eliminated, but it can be diverted. Our concern with the money supply has been diverted into a concern about consumer price increases. This diversion is so persistent that it even spills into the dictionary.

I have a Webster's dictionary from 1920, and another from 2006. Look at the difference in the definition of "inflation":

- the increased issue of paper currency (1920)
- a continuing rise in the general price level (2006)

We are told to be concerned with consumer prices, and the government reports consumer prices to us with the Consumer Price Index (CPI). Because the government interferes with the market so much, reporting consumer prices is complicated. Amidst these complications completely fraudulent adjustments are made in calculation methods and reporting, and they slip in virtually undetected.

I'll explain more about that later.

CPI is so confusing that no consumer would attempt to understand it. Instead, experts and analysts come together to agree that CPI is a useful measure of inflation. Social Security benefits, life insurance payouts and all kinds of financial instruments rely on CPI to adjust for inflation. They can't all be wrong, a naive consumer presumes.

First, remember they are measuring prices, not inflation. If we want to know how much inflation there is, we needn't go any further than the inflator—the Fed.

"Hey, how much money are you printing over there?" we would ask them.

"It's all right here in our report," they would reply.

Then experts, analysts, and economists would have their sought-after inflation figure.

But this type of candor doesn't exist today. Instead of keeping our eye on the ball, our attention is diverted to prices, prices are manipulated through government interference, and report calculations are further manipulated to create an utterly worthless CPI figure.

Ebb and Ebb

This dollar that we all work for, spend, save, and invest—is changing value all the time. Unfortunately, these changes don't go in both directions. Televised financial discussions claim that the dollar is changing value by showing us currency markets where the dollar is up with a green arrow one day and down with a red arrow the next. Most people believe it's an ebb and flow.

The fact is that the dollar has lost 95 percent of its value since 1971. That's no ebb and flow. It's a persistent decline that matches the Fed's persistent printing of money. If a green arrow shows up on your TV screen tomorrow to tell you the dollar is gaining value, does your milk go down in price that day? What about your utility bill? Does your rent or mortgage payment go down?

The red and green arrow game is one played by traders in a land far, far away. These guys borrow money from other people (often us), and use ridiculous amounts of leverage to enter positions for short periods of time, often hours or even minutes. It's outright gambling. One trader will win for a few months or years until his luck changes—his Lamborghini gets repossessed and his house foreclosed. Then another trader will buy that Lamborghini at auction and let the bankrupted fellow sleep on his couch.

Why the news reports the results of this currency market casino to us I can't tell you. But I do know that your real-life experience is completely disconnected from the red and green arrow game. Watching the game just distracts you from the real currency situation that affects you—the debasement of the dollar.

Let's get back to your bank and portfolio statements. Whether it's a CD, savings account, IRA, or 401(k), you look at the bottom line. The balance. The value.

But you aren't looking at the value at all. You're looking at the price, as measured in dollars. This means nothing. If your 401(k) grew from $100,000 to $700 million in the next 5 years, would you be satisfied?

It depends. If a club sandwich costs $900 million, your $700 million 401(k) probably wouldn't be considered immense wealth. Do you see yet? You don't want dollars. You want the stuff dollars buy.

Now we're getting to the root of the matter, and it's surprisingly uncomplicated.

Inflation can't be forecast, because we have no idea what the clowns at the Federal Reserve are going to do next. If inflation can't be forecast, you can't rationally set goals for your future as measured in dollars because that wouldn't be a goal at all.

This point bears repeating. You don't want dollars—you want the stuff dollars buy.

I will offer you a measurement solution. It won't be perfect, but it will be infinitely more useful as a unit of measurement than the dollar.

CHAPTER FOUR

CREATING YOUR OWN PERSONAL CURRENCY

Creating and maintaining your own personal currency will cost a few hundred dollars per year. The flip side is that the other four steps will save you thousands or possibly even millions of dollars.

To start, make a list of the things you might buy between now and the rest of your life. The list doesn't have to be perfect. Just make one. Here's what mine looks like:

- Food (bananas, grapefruit, oranges, carrots, cans of organic soup)
- Sushi restaurant dinners consisting of 12 pieces of Nigiri, one California roll, and green tea
- Flights to international target destinations (Singapore, Hong Kong, Tokyo, Thailand, Sweden, Peru, Argentina, Brazil, Belize, Costa Rica, Panama)

- Homes for purchase in international target destinations
- Homes for rent in international target destinations
- Hotel rates in international target destinations
- Flights from Denver to domestic target destinations (New York, Los Angeles, Atlanta, Seattle, San Francisco, San Diego, Myrtle Beach, San Antonio)
- Homes for purchase in domestic target destinations
- Homes for rent in domestic target destinations
- Hotel rates in domestic target destinations
- Home energy in target destinations
- Home water in target destinations
- Cell phones
- Unlimited cell phone usage
- Season pass ski lift tickets to Vail Resorts
- Gym membership to Denver Athletic Club
- Gasoline
- Concert tickets
- Gibson Les Paul guitars
- Songs on iTunes
- Movie theater tickets

As you can see, I plan to travel to my heart's content. Your list will be based on your plans. If you're a pro wakeboarder, you may want to pick a certain wakeboarding boat. If you're a golfer, list the golf courses you want to play.

Add gold and silver to the list.

Next, pick a unit of purchase for each of these items. For example, a gallon for gasoline, an ounce for gold, a kilowatt hour for home energy, unlimited monthly airtime for a cell phone, round trip tickets for flights, a pound for fruit or other foods, etc.

Now, it's time to make a fraction. Don't worry, we're sticking with easy math that anyone with a calculator can do. Our aim is to create a unit of measurement that starts out equal to about $1,000 USD. We'll start with gold and silver.

1/X   [purchase unit of]   [item]   = $_______ USD

So with gold…

1/3 ounce of gold = $300 USD

To get that figure, I looked up the price of an ounce of gold on goldprice.com. It was $900 (I'm rounding for easy numbers). Then I divided that by the number that replaced "X". In this case I divided $900 by 3 to get $300.

Now with silver…

1/1 pound of silver = $224 USD

I looked up the price of an ounce of silver. It was $14. Gold and silver should each make up a significant piece of any personal currency, so I used a pound (16 ounces) for silver. I multiplied $14 (price per ounce) by 16 to arrive at silver's price per pound, which is $224. Then I divided by 1, which of course leaves it at $224.

I'm going to aim for my personal currency unit to be equal to about $1,000 USD. The gold and silver calculations already total $524, so I have $476 left to attribute to the other items on my lifetime consumption list.

After finding the purchase unit of each item on my lifetime consumption list, I will tweak and adjust the "X" in the equation to my liking. All of the remaining items will need to add up to about $476, so it will take a bit of tweaking. For each item's equation, a larger USD figure on the right side of the equal sign will indicate more importance, while a smaller USD figure will indicate less. As I'm tweaking my figures, I'll increase the value of "X" to get a lower USD figure and I'll decrease the value of "X" to get a higher USD figure.

To download a spreadsheet to automatically do the math for you as you create and track your personal currency, visit FiveStepsToFreedomBook.com.

Your end result will be a spreadsheet that lists your lifetime consumption items in certain measurements that add up to about $1,000 dollars. It doesn't have to be exact, but try to get within $100 of a $1,000 total.

Viola! You now have a personal currency. I'll call mine "Jeff Bucks". Name yours whatever you like. You could use a generic, descriptive name like "My Personal Currency". So $1 MPC = $1,000 USD. It doesn't matter that each unit of MPC is equal to a thousand dollars because you're not going to print MPC cash and try to use it to pay for things. You'll just use MPC to measure your savings and wealth. This spreadsheet you've made to create your MPC will contain your MPC conversion rate. Initially, this conversion rate will be about 1,000.

Your First
Meaningful Financial Statement

To make a balance sheet, start with a piece of paper with two columns. On the left, list all of your assets, but convert their value to MPC. Then list all of your liabilities, converted to MPC, on your right. Subtracting your liabilities from your assets will show you your net worth. Let's take a look at what this would look like with conventional holdings.

Balance Sheet[1]					
Assets	**USD**	**MPC**	**Liabilities**	**USD**	**MPC**
House	300,000	300.00	Mortgage	190,000	190.00
Car	21,000	21.00	Car loan	6,400	6.40
Savings account	50,000	50.00			
Securities portfolio	125,000	125.00			
Total Assets	496,000	496.00	Total Liabilities	196,400	196.40
Net Worth	299,600	299.60	*(MPC conversion rate: 1,000)*		

---

[1] This is a simplified version of a balance sheet. You can download a complete balance sheet template at FiveStepsToFreedomBook.com.

Your first MPC financial statement will look just like a dollar-based financial statement, except the MPC figures will be divided by 1,000. That's because it's a starting point snapshot.

Updating Your Personal Currency

Over time, $1 MPC will equal more than $1,000 USD.

In the short term, it's possible that it could equal less than $1,000 USD as the global financial bubble corrects itself, but the longer-term movement will bring inflation as long as the Fed continues its 25-year habit of inflating the money supply. Regardless of the movement, using MPC won't affect what you have—it will only measure it.

As time passes, $1 MPC will equal a larger and larger amount of USD. To track this, you'll need to open your spreadsheet and update the USD price of each item on your list. For example, if gold rose to $1,000 per ounce, the spreadsheet would be updated to show:

1/3 ounce of gold = $333 USD

Update each line on your spreadsheet. This is where the cost comes in, in the form of either time or money. If you don't want to spend the time looking up USD prices for each line item, hire a virtual assistant to do it for you. You can Google "virtual assistant" and find plenty of people ready to perform tasks for you at a rate of $15 per hour or less. Updating your MPC might take 5 to 10 hours, depending on how detailed your list is. If you paid a virtual assistant to look up the prices and update your spreadsheet, it would cost around $75 to $150. I recommend updating your MPC quarterly, which would cost $300 to $600 per year.

The result of each quarterly MPC report will be an updated conversion rate. It will fill in the blank for "$1 MPC = $____ USD". The figure in that blank will be your MPC conversion rate.

Using Your Personal Currency

Remember, you're not going to print up and attempt to circulate MPC cash because federal agents would promptly arrest you. Instead, your MPC will be used to correct your financial statements so you can measure what you have.

Go back to your balance sheet to re-enter the USD values of your assets and liabilities. Include everything you own, such as your house, car, bank accounts, etc. Then enter in your updated liabilities, such as balances on mortgage loans, car loans, etc. They should all be entered in USD.

Then convert them to MPC using your latest conversion rate, and your updated balance sheet will show your net worth. I recommend you prepare an MPC balance sheet every 3 months, but you can do it more often if you'd like to keep a closer watch over what you have.

Measuring your net worth in meaningful terms with MPC will be an eye opener. Let's take the first balance sheet example and update it as if the MPC conversion rate rose to

1,200. This means we would divide each USD figure by 1,200 to arrive at its MPC equivalent.

Balance Sheet					
Assets	**USD**	**MPC**	**Liabilities**	**USD**	**MPC**
House	300,000	250.00	Mortgage	188,000	156.67
Car	20,400	17.00	Car loan	6,000	5.00
Savings account	51,000	42.00			
Securities portfolio	127,000	105.83			
Total Assets	498,400	415.33	Total Liabilities	194,000	161.67
Net Worth	304,400	253.67			
Previous Net Worth	299,600	299.60			
Net Worth Change	+4,800	-45.93	*(MPC conversion rate: 1,200)*		
Net Worth Change %	+1.60%	-15.33%			

This updated balance sheet reflects the fact that you paid down your loans a little bit, added to your savings account, and experienced a rise in the USD price of your securities portfolio. Deceptively measured in dollars, you've increased your net worth by $4,800 or 1.60 percent. The underlying truth is in MPC. You've actually lost $46.44 MPC or 15.50 percent of your holdings.

Imagine you started doing this in 1971. You started with $100 MPC ($100,000 USD). Assume you kept it all in cash in a safe—what you believed to be the safest haven. A balance sheet produced today would show that you have around $5 or $10 MPC left, down from $100 MPC.

What's more, the Fed's printing presses are running in high gear like never before. The money supply is increasing at rates we have never experienced.

Let's not ignore what today's experts would say.

"The stock market is a great hedge for inflation."

While the stock market would have outperformed sticking cash in a safe in our scenario above, it still fails to break even. Instead of having $5 MPC left over, you would have $55 MPC. A 45 percent loss over a period of 31 years leaves something to be desired.

That's right. You read it correctly. The highly acclaimed lengthy "bull market" in stocks was mostly inflationary. It was price increases with no value increases.

Furthermore, all rational indications say that, from this point forward, the stock markets will not even be able to perform as well as they have in the past. Which is why you must...

STEP 2: MOVE

CHAPTER FIVE

DUMPING THE DOOMED

Move. No, I don't mean pack your bags and prepare to leave the U.S. I mean move your money.

Get completely out of the stock market!

The stock market is literally nothing more than a casino and chances are you aren't the house. Try to trade individual stocks. You will win some and lose some. You will attribute your wins to your stock-picking skills and shrug off your losses because "Hey, I won before. I can do it again, right?"

Yes, there is a tiny minority of individual investors who make money trading individual stocks, just as there is a tiny minority of professional gamblers who profit in casinos. But the vast majority of people who have tried this (both in stock markets and casinos) have given up because they've lost too much (or even all) of their money.

Back in 1968, less than 25 percent of American households owned stocks. The stock market was viewed as a place where rich people gambled. Today, less than 25 percent of American households *don't* own stock. What happened?

As you already know, the Fed was able to start its printing presses in 1971. In addition to that, a tax law combined with a demographic anomaly poured fuel onto the fire of stock market hopes and celebrations.

The Two-Way Boomer Vacuum

When tax-favored retirement accounts were created in 1974, Wall Street took notice and heavily marketed the IRA. When 401(k) plans were created in 1981, Wall Street marketed even harder. The tax advantages of this kind of retirement account are enormous. Under the current system, taxes are your single biggest expense in your lifetime, so deferring or eliminating some of them is a no-brainer. As a result, in the 1970s, 1980s, and 1990s, the popularity of these retirement accounts soared, and over 99 percent of the accounts were set up automatically to buy Wall Street and banking investment products only. This tax law sucked a huge amount of money into the stock market.

Massive retirement account contributions by Baby Boomers created an upward trend in the stock market that conventional wisdom assumed would last forever. For this actually to occur, however, the people who make up this most populous generation would have to live forever, continuing to contribute to their retirement funds and never withdrawing and spending any of their money.

That's not going to happen. The Baby Boomers are beginning to cease making retirement account contributions,
and this will bring an end to the massive buying of stocks
that we have grown accustomed to. Furthermore, those same
Baby Boomers whose money was sucked into the stock market by tax law incentives will begin sucking their money
right back out of their retirement funds to pay for their living expenses in their retirement years. This will require *selling*. The same force that appeared to push the stock market
magically upward for decades will cause it to come crashing
drastically downward as Boomers retire.

Funny Funds

Another key factor in the stock market's popularity has
been mutual funds, index funds, and the most recent development, exchange-traded funds. It wasn't very easy to convince people to buy stocks when nobody, professionals or
laymen, could pick the stocks that go up and avoid the
stocks that go down.

So Wall Street cranked it up a notch on the cleverness
scale and said, "Buy into this mutual fund. It is diversified.
Some things may go down while others go up, but you will
be protected by our diversification." The moment Americans
bought into this scheme was a historical turning point.

Wall Street promoters realized that Americans were willing to buy… well nothing in particular. An investor who has
invested in a mutual fund has no idea what he just invested

in. Yes, the fund manager produces a list of the types of assets he holds, but this is a mere snapshot taken every quarter. That's four days per year. He can buy and sell whatever he wants during the other 361 days per year.

A fund manager can make a killing by taking large risks. After all, he's only risking *other people's money*. If he loses the money, he'll get fired and be forced to take a job that pays him seven figures per year instead of eight. And if the fund manager looks like he's about to get fired because of poor fund performance... well, he'll just have to swing for the fences with extraordinary risks—with other people's money.

After a while, reports started surfacing that said the vast majority of mutual funds don't even outperform the stock indexes. These fund managers were supposed to be wizards who could pick more above-average stocks and fewer below-average stocks and diversify away the risk. But these reports indicated that most mutual funds were performing so poorly that the simple act of buying *all* the stocks yielded better results.

Enter index funds. Not everybody can afford to buy every stock in a stock index. But alas, now we all can. And even better for Wall Street promoters, there's no fund manager to compensate. It takes no expertise to pool a bunch of money together and buy every stock with it. A computer will do that for free.

Meanwhile, as all of these "investment solutions" were being promoted, Americans were becoming a bit too comfortable with not even knowing what they just invested in. Can we all have faith in any old shmoe who happens to get his company traded on a stock exchange? Does every S&P 500 index fund investor really like all 500 companies so much that he wants to own all of them?

Of course not.

How do so many people get convinced to buy into... well whatever their money went to buy? Lots of marketing, twisting, spinning, and when all else fails, lying...

Lying Averages

Have you ever heard the phrase, "numbers don't lie?" Oh, yes they do. Let me show you how. Say four different investment portfolios start at the same time with the same amount of money. They experience different gains and losses each year, but they all have the same average return over the same period of time. Would they perform the same during that period of time? No.

Many people believe that a portfolio having an average return of 8 percent means that it performs the same as if it had experienced actual returns of 8 percent each year. This simply isn't true. It's a fuzzy assumption that runs contrary to the actual math. If two portfolios are compared during a period of time in which both have the same *average* return but one has losses, the portfolio without the losses will out-perform the other, even though they both have the same average return. What does this mean for you? It means that if you invest during turbulent times when your portfolio loses value in a year, you may find it impossible to get your real life investment returns to match up with the shiny, jazzy reports (and hopes) your financial planner gave you many years ago.

What most people call average stock market returns is what I call a "lying average." Technically, it's the "simple average" or "arithmetic mean," but if you believe it is meaningful in real world investing, you'll be wrong. If your investments went up 100 percent one year, and then lost 50 percent the next year, you'd be back where you started. But if you average the rates of return, the average return computes to 25 percent ([+100% - 50%] ÷ 2)! That's how *lying averages* work. They almost always *overstate* the real average return, which is the "geometric mean," or the "Compound Annual Growth Rate" (CAGR). The real return in this example is zero. You doubled your money, and then you halved it, netting a real return of zero.

If your investment portfolio matched the performance of the S&P 500 (which most mutual funds aren't even able to do), your investments would be drastically short of what most Wall Street pundits told you.

To illustrate, let's look at some real data from the S&P 500 index.

Real and Compound Annual Growth Rates

Date Range: 1968 – 2008

Average return	7.09%
True CAGR	5.57%
Standard deviation	17.15%

Date Range: 1998 - 2008

Average return	1.49%
True CAGR	-0.65%
Standard deviation	19.80%

Let's examine the hypothetical case of William. Suppose he invested $100,000 into the stock market in 1968. He used a retirement account to defer all taxation. (Even though "defined contribution" retirement accounts didn't exist then, let's assume they did to keep this example simple). He expected a return of 7.09 percent over the long term. Forty years later, he takes a look at the average returns of his investments and they are stated as exactly 7.09 percent when measured by the arithmetic mean. So, he was successful, right?

Not exactly. William checks his math and finds that a 7.09 percent return should have resulted in a 2008 account balance of $1,554,457. William is baffled when he looks at his IRA statement because he sees only $884,213. "Where's the rest of my money?" he shouts at his self-proclaimed financial planner. "I don't know," replies the financial planner, just as confused as William.

His true CAGR is 5.57 percent. It's only a couple percentage points lower than the target 7.09 percent, but it makes a world of difference when compounded over many years. To be exact, he has fallen 43 percent short of his target retirement balance!

William's Shortfall

Starting point 1968	$100,000
2008 goal using arithmetic mean	$1,554,457
2008 reality	$884,213
Missing money $	$670,244
Missing Money %	43.12%

With an actual retirement balance of only about half his target fund balance, there seems to be little William can do to rectify the situation. If he retired now, William would have to live on much less money than he had expected from the Wall Street sales pitch and the lying averages.

The Boomer vacuum and lying averages are reason enough to get out of the stock market. The immense amount of outright, blatant fraud within the stock market is not even mentioned as there are many books devoted to it. Even if all three of these reasons didn't exist, the bigger picture shows us that the long-term rise in stock market prices can be credited to inflation. The stock market is clearly no place to win. Get out now.

When considering a full exit from the stock market, many people assume their IRA & 401(k) accounts must be distributed, which is a taxable event. This isn't so. We'll cover more on that later.

STEP 3: MAINTAIN

CHAPTER SIX

KEEPING WHAT YOU HAVE

Maintaining, or saving, is part of the life plan society prescribes:

1. Go to work to make money
2. Spend less than your earn
3. Save and/or invest the remainder of your earnings for your future

As the next decade unfolds, many Americans will lose almost everything they have with conventional savings—CDs, money market funds, and savings accounts. The worst part is they won't even know what has happened until it's too late. Let's have a preview of what will happen if you ignore this book's prescription and change nothing. But first...

A Primer On Money

For most of human history, gold and silver served as money. We started out bartering and then discovered the need for a medium of exchange. We experimented with shells and other objects, but found that they were too abundant. Precious metals became the most popular form of money because there is a finite amount of them on and in planet earth.

Eventually, gold depositories emerged as a place to store gold and receive a paper certificate (deposit receipt). People started using these paper certificates as money because it was easier than carrying gold around. Those issuing the paper certificates soon realized additional paper certificates could be created without a real gold deposit. Pushing the envelope, societies eventually experimented with trading paper only, without gold or silver backing. This is known as *fiat currency*.

Fiat currency has been used repeatedly throughout history, yet it has always failed. The flaw is that the organization responsible for printing and regulating the paper money (the central bank) holds a power ripe for abuse. Without abuse, fiat currency would theoretically work fine. Unfortunately, that has yet to happen. The abuse happens when the central bank rapidly prints additional fiat money, which dilutes the purchasing power of that money.

In the United States, the Federal Reserve is the organization that creates and regulates money. Many people are not aware that the Fed is not a government agency; it is owned by a group of (mostly foreign) private bankers. Although there are mounds of evidence of this, the most recent proof came when the news network Bloomberg sued the Fed to disclose information under the Freedom of Information Act about who it lent $2 trillion to. That law requires government agencies to disclose information when requested. Bloomberg was shocked to find out that the Fed isn't subject to the Freedom of Information Act because it isn't a government agency.

Not surprisingly, the Fed has often abused its power. We're in somewhat of a pickle because neither taxpayers nor Congress exercise significant authority or control over the Fed. We don't elect those who run it, and they don't publicly report much about their operations.

The Fed used to publish data about precisely how it's been fooling with our money supply, but in 2006 it stopped publishing M3 money supply data because—*get this*—"It's too expensive and nobody needs the information." Are you finished laughing?

The Rug To Sweep M3 Under

The Fed's ceasing to publish M3 isn't the big problem. In fact, hardly anybody noticed they stopped publishing the broadest report on the money supply. When M3 was still being published, it was just swept under the rug of CPI. As mentioned earlier, we've been told to forget about the money supply and only be concerned with price inflation as reported by the Consumer Price Index—which has been out of touch with reality since the 1990s.

CPI is meant to tell us how much consumer prices are rising or falling. In the 1990s, the method of calculating and reporting CPI was effectively changed to a figure that represents how much consumers are spending. *Prices* may double, but *spending* can't double without an increase in consumer income or borrowing. Tying CPI to consumer spending allows inflation to soar into double digits while the "official" CPI is reported at 3 percent to 5 percent. I call this post-1990's CPI "**fauxflation.**"

In the fauxflation corner, there are many arguments and seeing through them will help you remove any doubt so that you can wholeheartedly move on to learning how to MAINTAIN what you have.

CHAPTER SEVEN

A CLOSER LOOK AT PRICE INFLATION

The most common explanations of the cause of price inflation can be extremely confusing. They often lead the reader/inquirer to conclude, *"Ah, it's just too complicated. We can't really put our finger on it, and there are so many different factors."*

Theory #1 - Demand-Pull Inflation

"Too much money is chasing too few goods." This is the theory that says inflation is caused when demand outpaces supply. Those who subscribe to this theory point to inflation as evidence of a growing economy. It's easy to conclude otherwise.

Imagine that demand for iPods skyrockets for some reason. The price of an iPod is increased by $50 as a result of the demand for iPods being greater than the supply. Foolish economists will say that this is all part of a growing economy and that rising iPod prices are contributing to inflation.

What they overlook is that the consumer who paid $50 extra for the iPod now has $50 less left over for spending on something else, such as shoes. His capacity to spend money on shoes has been reduced by precisely the amount he increased his spending for the iPod. Looking at the whole market, the increased demand for iPods, which results in a higher price, is made possible only by an equal decrease in demand for other goods.

In reality, the $50 rise in price for the iPod won't result in an easy-to-see $50 decrease in the price of shoes, but it will produce smaller price decreases in a wide variety of other goods. This is because each iPod buyer will make his own unique decision about where to decrease spending as a result of paying the higher price for the iPod. The demand-pull inflation theory exists because price inflation is not as simple as an inverse iPod-shoe price relationship. Yet the large, complex economy is just huge collection of transactions. Looking at an individual transaction shows us that the higher iPod price simply creates lower prices for the other goods from which demand was diverted.

Conclusion: False.

Theory #2 - Cost-Push Price Inflation

"When their costs go up, companies have to raise prices to maintain a profit margin." This may explain isolated price fluctuations, but price inflation is the steady rise in the price of goods in general. A more fundamental question is this: What is causing the companies' costs to go up? The Cost-Push Inflation theory is almost like saying, "Rising prices are caused by rising prices." Huh? **Conclusion: False.**

Supply and demand of goods has nothing to do with inflation. Consider the rising price of oil, from the perspective of the Demand-Pull and Cost-Push theories. Whether it's because of an increase in demand, a decrease in supply, or a combination of both, Americans who spend more money at the gas pump have less left over for buying jewelry and dining out. The price of jewelry and restaurant dining will go down because demand for them is lower as a result of increases in the price of oil. The net effect is that in the "basket of goods" inflation calculation, oil prices rise while the prices of other items decline. Price inflation is thus generally unaffected by demand-pull and cost-push mechanisms.

Theory #3 - Monetary Inflation

Imagine that everyone wakes up tomorrow with twice the amount of money they have today. Companies that sell goods and services will discover that we will bear higher prices. This will cause prices to double eventually. If this happens one time, it isn't price inflation per se, because it's not continual. But if this happens every night, price inflation will follow.

Unfortunately for American citizens (and anyone who earns or spends in dollars), this monetary debasement doesn't merely happen because each of us wakes up every morning with more money. It happens because of two central banking phenomena that put that new money into the hands of some people and not others.

Phenomenon # 1 – The Fed's Digital Printing. In our economy, we use money created by a private bank, the Federal Reserve (Fed). When we came off the gold standard in 1971, the ties between money and commodities were severed. Since that time, most money has simply been a blip on a financial statement, and more recently, a blip in cyberspace. There is an endless supply of blips and their paper equivalents. Whoever has the authority to increase the amount of blips has more power than the government itself, because even the government has to earn and spend its money denominated in those blips too. That unlimited authority is in the hands of the Fed.

Example: The Fed buys $50 million worth of U.S. bonds from a member bank, *ABC Bank*. The Fed credits ABC bank with money for the sale of the U.S. bonds. What account does this come from? A magical one. *ABC Bank* is *credited* with $50 million, but there is no corresponding Fed account that is debited $50 million. This is the Fed "printing money." People talk all the time about how the Fed *could* print money, but few realize it's actually happening constantly, and price inflation is evidence of it.

Phenomenon # 2 - Fractional Reserve Banking

Another equally magical way money is created is through fractional reserve banking. In this system, we can borrow money that doesn't exist. If you deposit $1 into a bank, about 9 additional dollars that did not previously exist can be lent out. The bank that actually has the original money is able to lend about 90 cents of your dollar out. When money is borrowed, it is usually deposited into another bank account, and then into yet another. Even if it is spent, the recipient of the money will normally also deposit it into his bank. The repeated multiplication process turns the originally deposited dollar into about 10 dollars. Our banking system allows money to be created whenever a person, corporation, or government borrows money from a bank. That money is then brought into circulation. The benefit of this price inflation multiplier is enjoyed only by a banking system that earns interest on the money created every time it is lent and borrowed.

Almost as important in monetary history as abandoning the gold standard was the 2006 Fed decision to stop publishing its M3 statistic. This was a report that told us how much new money was created each year. Its last report (around March 2006) said that our money supply was increasing by about 8 percent per year. Independent sources have subsequently attempted to mimic M3 reports. These have reported annual money supply increases of between 8 percent and 16 percent.

Simply put: monetary inflation (an increasing money supply) creates price inflation.

What is the current rate of price inflation?

This is where there is a difference of opinion. For decades, price inflation was estimated using a "basket of goods" approach. In this method, the price of each of a variety of goods was tracked, a logical weighting was applied, and the output was the rate of price inflation, usually annualized. Under this method, we could see price inflation swinging up and down through economic cycles. In the early 1980s, this data showed price inflation at nearly 15 percent per year, according to the published figures of the U.S. Bureau of Labor Statistics (BLS).

However, in the early 1990s, the methodology of price inflation reporting changed drastically, rendering the BLS' "official" figures virtually useless. Unfortunately, these BLS figures continue to be used as if they were accurate.

Changes in calculation methods: Around 1993, Alan Greenspan and others sought and received new ways to calculate price inflation. Since this change in methodology, the BLS has been reporting price inflation at between 2 and 5 percent per year, through all the economic cycles of the past decade. For the first time it appears, on the surface at least, that we've conquered the laws of economics. Independent economists have continued to estimate price inflation using the methodology in effect prior to the substitution change. They estimate price inflation fluctuated between 7 and 13 percent between 1996 and 2008.[2] It appears that the new methods consistently misreport price inflation data by up to 200 percent. Let's explore how these adjustments work.

---

[2] See shadowstats.com

CHAPTER EIGHT

THE MAKINGS OF FAUXFLATION

While the measurement of price inflation varies wildly depending on which economist you talk to, here we will examine the Consumer Price Index (CPI), the official index published by the BLS. The CPI is supposed to measure inflation and/or deflation, the decreased or increased buying power of the U.S. dollar. Understanding inflation essentially means understanding how much our central banking system, the Federal Reserve, is destroying the value of money through "monetary policy." This side of economics can get confusing, but it doesn't have to be. This account will be an understandable explanation intended for accountants and laymen alike.

CPI is not calculated the same today as it was in the '70s and '80s. While remarkably high inflation is central to our memory of the '70s and '80s, if today's CPI calculation methods were applied to the '70s and'80s, the CPI figures would show very low inflation—probably under 6 percent. Why? Two important concepts have altered today's CPI calculation method, one of which is *hedonics*.

CPI Hedonics Adjustments

Hedonic means "relating to usefulness" or more literally "relating to pleasure."

CPI is calculated using a "basket of goods" approach. This means that the BLS figures out the most common goods that American consumers purchase, puts them into a virtual basket, and assesses how much more or less that basket costs each year. That's it.

Over time, politicians have argued that such a simple approach is flawed, and some of these arguments have resulted in altering the BLS policy of how to calculate and report CPI.

The hedonics argument says that one must look at the increased usefulness of goods over time and expect increased usefulness to bring increased prices with it. The more useful something is, the more you would expect it to cost, and this expectation "deserves" to be factored into CPI calculations. Utility is basically a function of technological advances. For example, if a computer is in the basket of goods, BLS tries to measure the price of a computer based on its usefulness. Ten years ago, a standard home computer would come with a 200MB hard drive. Today, a standard home computer would be more likely to come with a 200 GB hard drive offering 1,000 times more data storage space. The hedonics adjustment says that today's computer should be much higher in price. But in the real world, the price of the computer is actually the same or lower, and BLS adjusts its price reports as if the price had gone down. This counteracts the other items in the basket of goods that went up in price.

Let's use a fictional example to take a look at this adjustment concept. Say we are tracking a very basic basket of goods. In this basket is only a home computer and gasoline, and imagine we normally spend an equal amount of money on each. Assume that since last year, gasoline has doubled, and the usefulness of the computer has doubled as well. The hedonics adjustment would adjust the computer price to half of last year's price because of its doubled usefulness. So this year's inflation calculation would report no inflation at all. Yet, in reality, where we citizens work, play, and balance our checkbooks, we are paying double last year's price for gasoline and the same price for computers. The actual adjustment is much more complicated, but the basic principle is the same.

Problem 1: Other causes of decreased prices and increased usefulness

Decreasing Prices - In the process of technological evolution, as new devices grow in popularity more people buy them. Increasing the quantity of devices manufactured usually decreases the per-unit cost of production. This is because fixed costs like research and development don't increase with increased production. This is usually referred to as "economies of scale". As a device grows in production and sales, its price also drops as a result of marketplace competition.

Increased usefulness - This isn't rocket science. We humans invent and innovate. This alone should not bring prices up, because competition brings prices down. The price of an item is somewhat tied to the price it costs to produce it. A business cannot perpetually sell goods for a lower price than its cost of production. So when production costs come down, competitors offer reduced prices. Innovation increases usefulness, but it also increases efficiency. The ultimate effect of innovation is more likely to be downward pressure on prices than upward pressure.

In fact there have been many times in history when a stable money supply resulted in mild deflation, thus creating deflationary booms.[3]

Problem 2: The hedonics adjustment doesn't go both ways

You know the saying "they don't make 'em like they used to." Although this isn't always the case, cheaper and less useful products do emerge. Many of today's products are of lower quality than yesterday's products. As more and more products are made in China and other countries with

---

[3] Thomas E. Woods, *Meltdown*, 135.

lower labor costs and overhead, we often discover that we need to replace them more often; they are of decreased usefulness. Yet there is no allowance for this phenomenon in the BLS hedonics adjustment.

The big picture

The BLS basically takes the position that our original, simple approach to CPI only works in a society where there is no innovation. But we are quite innovative, and technological advances in our society are actually substantial and rapid. To adjust for this, the BLS pretends that every year electronic equipment costs less than it actually does. Hence, the CPI no longer represents price inflation in the real world. Instead, it represents price inflation in an imaginary world where you can go to the store, select a computer that costs $1000, pay $1000 to buy it, and somehow only have $500 debited from your pocket.

CPI Substitution Adjustments

The BLS CPI calculation policies were altered in a second major way. The concept of *substitution* assumes that as the price of an item rises, consumers start buying cheaper alternatives.

To say that consumer substitution happens is absolutely true. It's a natural result of inflation. We know when things we buy go up in price. Everything doesn't go up equally at precisely the same time. As prices rise, we substitute goods to get the best deal. BLS uses this concept to **reduce the ma-**

thematical **weighting** of those items in the basket of goods that rise sharply in price. It assumes that when things rise in price, we seek alternatives that are not rising as rapidly in price, and we remain satisfied as a result. It thus turns logic on its head by assuming we consumers are "satisfied" because we seek out alternatives.

The real reason we seek alternatives is that we have to. When our incomes don't rise and prices do, something has to give. We have to figure out a way to make do. The BLS uses that evidence of "satisfaction" to justify ignoring the *actual* price increases. Perhaps nothing short of price inflation riots can overturn the BLS's opinion that we are "satisfied."

Since 1998, the concept of a "satisfied consumer" has completely altered the meaning of the CPI. **CPI no longer measures rising prices... it measures rising consumer spending.** Prices may rise by 50 percent in a year, but consumers with stagnant incomes cannot increase their spending by an equal amount. Instead, consumers experience a declining standard of living.

Consumer substitution *is a sign* of price inflation. The BLS has been convinced by politicians to use consumer substitution as justification for removing price inflation from price inflation. Huh? **The CPI is a way to "measure" price inflation without fully considering items that are rising rapidly in price.**

Think of it in the simple terms of a math equation like "2 + 2 = 4." On one side of the equation is the calculation, and on the other side is the result of the calculation. Measurements of price inflation should use an absolute formula on the left side of the equation to output an accurate figure on the right side. Unfortunately, the substitution adjustment to CPI has made it public policy to manipulate the left side of the equation so that the right side always reads 6 percent or less. Ever since these ridiculous adjustments were made to policy in the early '90s, CPI has never been reported above 6 percent. In fact, CPI will likely *never* be reported above 6 percent in the future, regardless of the dollar's decline and rising consumer prices, as long as these silly adjustments remain in place.

The Government Explanation

Visit FiveStepsToFreedomBook.com for links to the official government pages that document the ridiculous concepts of hedonics and substitution. They are not nearly as straightforward as what you have read here; instead, what they are talking about in these documents is hidden in boring, lengthy, technical, gobbledygook language. But nevertheless it is there for the edification of anyone who doubts the unreliability of official CPI figures. Here are some more of the "official" explanations:

<u>SSA Boskin Report</u> - This was a report from the Social Security Administration. It purported that CPI was overstated and suggested many complex, new adjustments to be put into practice for CPI calculations. Never mind that the SSA didn't have any of the money it was supposed to use to

pay future benefits and had an enormous incentive to cover up its insolvency.

<u>Gramlich's Congressional Testimony</u> - Governor Edward Gramlich testified to the House of Representatives on the topic of recent "improvements" in CPI calculations, but then pled for "substitution bias" to be "corrected." This testimony was the force behind getting substitution adjustments in place and shifting CPI to a *spending* report instead of a price report.

<u>BLS Handbook of Methods</u> - In this document, the BLS basically uses fancy terms and confusing, complex language to explain how the calculations are done, including "hedonics" and "substitution bias."

All of these government documents accuse that CPI is being *overstated* for various complex and obscure reasons. These testimonies and reports have resulted in alterations to the calculation policies. No government documents or reports or testimony I've seen complain that inflation is being *understated*. The result of all these many complex arguments has been that, over time, calculation methods have been reformed in ways that *reduce* the reported CPI but never in ways that *increase* the reported CPI.

Misreporting helps to balance the budget

It's also important to recognize that the government's own finances have unquestionably become a growing mess. With its debt rising much faster than income, the government is on a one-way path to bankruptcy, and there's not a single person on the planet who can convincingly argue otherwise. Anything government can do to minimize its expenses will help defer the financial reckoning. One side effect of CPI misreporting is that increases in social security payouts do not keep up with price inflation, based on the understated BLS inflation figures. CPI or "fauxflation" helps to lower government expenses, albeit dubiously.

Fauxflation and You

With fauxflation your investment portfolio could be showing 8 percent annual returns (which sounds like a dream in light of the current stock market conditions). However, sadly, it may take you 25 years to realize you've been tricked. Let's look at an example of what happens when the dollar is used as the primary method of wealth measurement and fauxflation reports are believed.

Robert has $100,000 in his taxable investment portfolio at the beginning of a 25-year period. He achieves 8 percent returns every year. CPI is *reported* at 4 percent each year, so Robert is happy that he is ahead of inflation. Unfortunately, the real but hidden price inflation was 15 percent. At the end of the 25 years, Robert is hungrier and poorer than when he started. "What happened?" he wonders. The cause is *invisible* to him. Table 1-2 below summarizes Robert's dilemma.

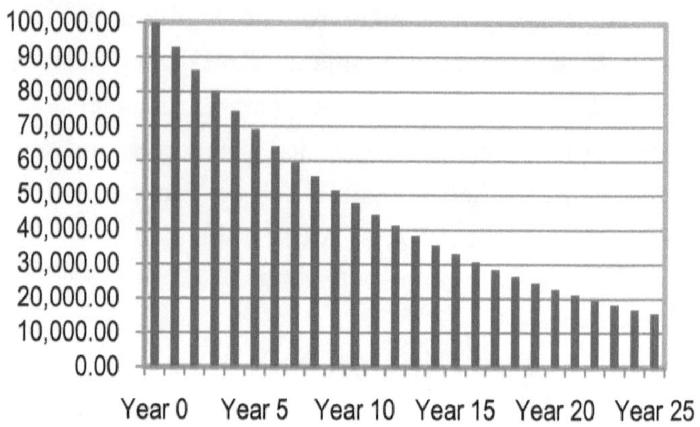

The decline in value of $100,000
over a period of 25 years at 15% inflation

Robert's loss of wealth was caused by his belief that "fauxflation" was true inflation. Real inflation was at 15 percent during those years, so he actually lost wealth every single year. Because he appeared to be growing his portfolio every year, the government taxed him accordingly. He might actually have $517,942 in his account at the end of the 25-year period, but that only would buy only the same amount of stuff as $15,722 did in the first year. Robert's eyes see that he more than quadrupled his money, but his stomach is grumbling and his family is starving. They are experiencing *invisible poverty*.

"But price inflation won't hit 15 percent in my lifetime," you argue. Think again. Our country saw 40 percent inflation in 1933. Economists saw *real* price inflation hit 13 percent in 2008[4]. Then, *trillions* of dollars were created in bailout packages. At the time of writing, trillions more are being created. As of January 2009, the monetary base was up 97.5 percent from the year before. All of this money won't be circulating in the economy until the fear subsides, but once it does, we may be wishing we were back in the "good ol' days" of 13 percent price inflation.

You may think it's impossible to maintain the value of what you have while inflation is 15 percent or higher, but, believe it or not, it is simple and easy.

---

[4] Visit shadowstats.com. Reports are listed under "alternate data."

CHAPTER NINE

SAFETY FIRST

Remember those good old Warner Bros. cartoons—that "wacky wabbit" and nutty Elmer Fudd? In one of the funniest episodes, Elmer Fudd is searching the desert for gold. "Eureka! Gold, at last!" He exclaims. But poor Elmer Fudd doesn't realize that he has been had, once again, by that screwy rabbit. The gold Elmer Fudd found comes from his own mouth… a shiny golden tooth! Ain't that rabbit a stinker!

When the cartoon was created in 1942, gold was still linked to the dollar. Today, as we saw earlier, we have a fiat money system that is not backed by gold.

This is damaging to the economy in many ways. As Congressman Ron Paul wrote in 2003, "History shows that when the destruction of monetary value becomes rampant, nearly everyone suffers and the economic and political structure becomes unstable. Spendthrift politicians may love a system that generates more and more money for their special interest projects, but the rest of us have good reason to be concerned about our monetary system and the future value of our dollars."

He also wrote, "Every dollar created dilutes the value of existing dollars in circulation. Those individuals who worked hard, paid their taxes, and saved some money for a rainy day are hit the hardest. Their dollars depreciate in value while earning interest that is kept artificially low by the Federal Reserve's easy-credit policy." Representative Paul's words, written several years ago, were prophetic. Anyone who understands the weaknesses of our monetary system seeks something tangible that can't be manipulated by any CEO, politician, or banker.

To those who don't understand how money works, it may appear that the volatile gold market has been bullish for nearly a decade because it saw a 30 percent rise in 2007 and has had double-digit gains for the last nine years. The price of gold has fluctuated over the decades from less than $35 per ounce to nearly $1,000 per ounce in recent years. But in reality, it is not gold that has been making big moves; it is the dollar. When the dollar loses value, gold holds its value. When gold doubles in dollar price, it still holds its value. It just takes twice as many dollars to buy the same ounce of gold. Many historians remark upon the consistency of what gold will buy. For instance, an ounce of gold would buy a tailored suit 100 years ago, and the same ratio holds roughly true today.

Additionally, the ratio of gold-to-oil has been fairly consistent for quite some time. In examining the chart that follows, you will notice that the ratio of both dollars-to-oil and gold-to-oil was quite constant from 1946 to 1972. Not long after the Fed got its license to print money without limits or oversights, the ratio of dollars-to-oil skyrocketed while the ratio of gold-to-oil remained stable.

Oil Priced in USD vs. Oil Priced in Gold Grams

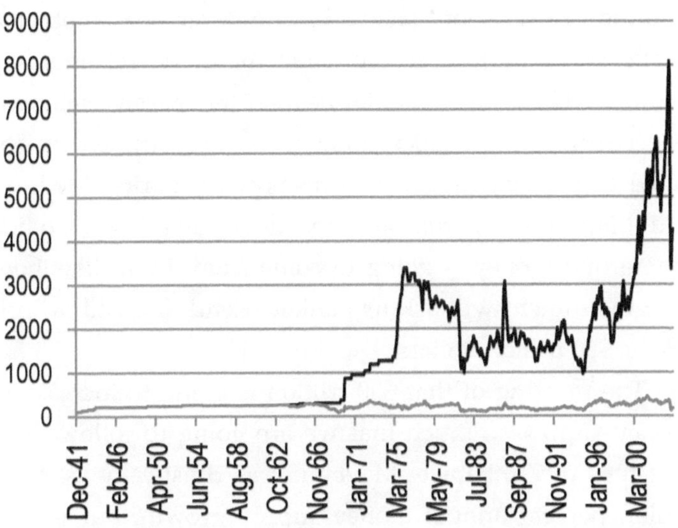

This chart shows the prices of gold and oil on an index where 100 represents their starting prices at the beginning of the time period.

The prospect of reaping real profits from gold isn't necessarily great, but its long-term value is consistent. As the Fed cranks up its printing press to unprecedented levels, maintaining the value of your MPC balance sheet is critical. The bailouts of banks, insurance companies, automobile manufacturers, and whoever gets the next round of handouts are ultimately funded with dollars that are created out of thin air. By early 2009, over $2 trillion had already been created from nothing. As all this new money creeps into our economy in the near future, your MPC conversion rate will skyrocket and you'll need to take measures to maintain your MPC balance.

"Well, we are bound to get ourselves out of this mess soon," says the optimist who has no meaningful unit of financial measurement. He hopes the Fed will downshift its printing presses soon. The realist, however, sees another gigantic wave of further economic madness: retiring Baby Boomers. Their effect goes far beyond the massive selling off of securities in the stock market. The government is obligated to pay over $50 trillion in Social Security, Medicare, and Medicaid benefits, and the government has no idea where that money is going to come from. In all likelihood, the government will ask its banker friend, the Fed, to print up the $50 trillion dollars.

The printing of that $50 trillion is going to increase the money supply so much that we are going to follow in the footsteps of Zimbabwe. Maybe not as drastically as its 658 billion percent annual money supply growth, but you are certain to see more inflation than you've ever experienced in your lifetime.

Meanwhile, the massive purchases of American treasuries by China may be coming to an end. China recently announced it has increased its gold holdings 75 percent since 2003 and is now pushing for a new world currency to replace the mismanaged dollar. While Secretary of Treasury Timothy Geithner publicly says that replacing the dollar with another reserve currency for the world is absolutely out of the question, he admitted to the Council of Foreign Relations that we are soon to "evolve" into a global currency regulated by a global central bank. The outlook for the dollar is not good. Any significant holdings in dollar-based bank accounts or the U.S. securities market will be annihilated. Those who recognize this fact will soon set their sights on gold and silver.

Replacing Bad Money With Good Money

Sir Thomas Gresham coined the phrase "bad money drives out good money." Known as Gresham's Law, this is a concept he used to explain to Queen Elizabeth why the English shilling had devalued because of the adulteration of the coin by Henry VIII, who had replaced 40 percent of the silver in the shillings with base metals and made them less valuable. People hoarded the good (higher purity level) silver shillings and circulated the shillings containing less silver.

Today, many people who are discouraged by the economy are protecting their wealth by buying and holding gold bullion in the form of bars or coins, which they can store wherever they choose. Gold mining stocks and exchange-traded funds (ETFs) allow you to buy shares of gold, but these are one step removed from being a tangible asset in your possession.

Forms of Gold Holdings

People who make money from selling ETFs tout them as the best way to invest in gold today, but with ETFs, you don't actually hold/own the gold. The ETFs are meant to reflect the actual price of gold but not to give actual owner-ship of gold to the investor. "At no time do you actually own a gold bar, bullion, or even a ring. Gold ETFs are made up of gold contracts and derivatives and can only be redeemed for cash, never gold itself," says Mark Kennedy, a writer who was an options trader on the Philadelphia Stock Exchange floor and a Vice President of Derivatives Trading for Gold-man Sachs.

He Who Holds The Gold

We all know the adage: "He who holds the gold makes the rules" or, at least in this case, maintains his holdings. So, let's explore physical possession of gold and how you can buy it.

In the old James Bond movie, *Goldfinger*, Bond is struck by a gold brick. That is how most people picture gold for investment. We picture large, rectangular-shaped, stamp-weighed gold bricks. But that's not necessarily the best way to buy and own gold. Those 400-ounce gold bars cost over $360,000 each at the time of this writing.

The often-preferred method of holding gold in North America and other parts of the world is in bullion coins. Gold has functioned as money for most of human history, but once gold was no longer linked to the dollar, gold coins were hoarded and became scarce and obsolete—more like collector's items.

Then, in 1967, South Africa introduced the Krugerrand, a one troy ounce, convenient, gold bullion coin that was government-issued and sold for the current spot price of gold plus a small percentage. The nominal face value ensured that any restrictions, duties, or taxes countries placed on raw gold bullion or legal tender could be avoided. Ironically, at the time of its release, it was illegal for Americans to own gold bullion. They could, however, own foreign coins.

Other countries such as Australia, Austria, Great Britain, and Singapore introduced similar gold coins with varying degrees of success. Today, other popular coins include Canadian Maple Leafs, Chinese Pandas, and American gold Eagles. All these gold coins guarantee purity, exact weight, and liquidity throughout the world. Holding physical possession of assets is vital in uncertain times. Later, we'll discuss how you can even hold these coins on behalf of your retirement account.

> Some coins are "numismatic," or have collector's value. Numismatic coins cannot be held inside a retirement account.

Don't expect to *become* rich through holding gold. Your holdings may skyrocket in dollars, but that's why it's important to measure in MPC. Not only does MPC reveal when conventional holdings go down, it also keeps your head level when your gold holdings are keeping a constant value.

Gold Storage & Transactions

Many precious metal dealers offer storage. When you buy from them you can choose to let them store your gold rather than take physical possession yourself. I am not much of a fan of this. If something major were to happen, such as China dumping its dollars, our economy would be in such upheaval that having your gold in someone else's storage facility might amount to having no gold at all. It makes more sense to *eliminate* the risk of losing your gold than it does to toil over deciding its severity.

Services such as GoldMoney.com have emerged as a precious metals dealer, storage facility, and transaction clearinghouse. You can buy gold or silver and take delivery, but you can also leave it in their storage facility, which is outside of the United States. An offshore storage facility is more confidence-inspiring than one onshore. GoldMoney takes things a step further and provides its customers the means to complete transactions with each other in gold or silver. One party can pay another in "gold grams" or "silver grams". It is essentially a matter of trading gold and silver certificates, but electronically.

The Threat of Confiscation

In discussions of gold ownership, the topic of government confiscation is often raised. It's ironic that some would challenge the idea of gold ownership based on a potential future confiscation of wealth when the standard practice of holding dollars involves constant, unremitting, methodical confiscation in the present.

Nevertheless, the topic deserves illumination.

The threat of confiscation is a concern primarily because of the previous government confiscation on April 5, 1933. It's commonly believed that the government somehow "took" all of the gold from the people. What really took place was more a "gold request" than anything else. The president signed an executive order[5] that requested U.S. citizens to deliver the majority of their gold to the nearest Federal Reserve branch bank in exchange for $20.67 in paper dollars for each troy ounce.

Reading through the history books provided to students of today's government-run schools may conjure up images of legions of obedient citizens lining up at Federal Reserve branches to surrender their gold to the almighty government. In reality… not so much.

People actually turned in 21.9% of the gold that was previously in circulation.[6] The government wrote off the remainder as lost or destroyed. If it was lost and destroyed at that point, then a few months later when gold ownership was allowed again, the same amount of gold was miraculously found and created.[7]

---

[5] An executive order is something that Presidents invented to give themselves powers not prescribed by the Constitution.

[6] *Monetary History of the United States* by Milton Friedman and Anna Schwartz, p.212.

[7] Despite the threat of imprisonment, there was only one case of government prosecution for failure to comply with Executive Order 6102. A federal judge ruled the case invalid on technical grounds and the prosecution against Frederick Barber Campbell, the defendant, failed. The federal government did, however, seize his gold.

Why was gold ownership prohibited and then allowed again? It was an inflationary move—the government wanted money to fund the "New Deal". When ownership was allowed again, the Treasury had raised the price of gold to $35 per ounce. Those who turned their gold into the Fed sold it at $20.67 and could later buy it back at $35 per ounce. Back then this type of drastic and obvious measure was necessary for the government to steal from its people because our money was linked to a physical commodity of limited supply, gold.

Could a big government confiscation happen again? A similar confiscation started in 1971 when Nixon closed the gold window and has been happening ever since. The difference is that the 1933 heist was a large amount of money in a small period of time—creating 40 percent inflation in a matter of months. Since the dollar was turned into a pure fiat currency in 1971, it has lost much more than 40 percent of its value, but in a slow and mostly continuous maneuver.

If you came home to a kicked-down door and all of your possessions were gone, you would be despondent. On the other hand, if the thief discreetly took only one item at a time only a couple of times per year, you wouldn't notice. Decades later, the thief may have stolen more than a home's worth of possessions from you in all, and yet you'd find it difficult to put your finger on the source of your financial troubles.

The 1933 gold request was like the thief who takes everything in one event. The monetary debasement that's been taking place since 1971 is the thief who inconspicuously steals from you gradually and repeatedly.

It is worth noting that there are many drastic measures being taken by government today. Obama essentially fired the CEO of private company, General Motors. Records are surfacing that the Department of Treasury practically forced Bank of America to purchase Merrill Lynch. Meanwhile, China is calling for a new global reserve currency to protect the world from our monetary shenanigans. If we reach a point where China's actions back its words, the dollar could completely crash. Then, government gold confiscation could be a threat.

But fear of being asked to surrender your gold shouldn't be a reason for not owning gold—it should be a reason for physically possessing gold. It is absolutely vital that you directly hold your assets without a financial institution being the middleman, *especially* your IRA & 401(k) assets, as discussed later. With physical possession, you make the choice on how you will react to your assets being targeted for theft.

Other mediums of maintaining

Physically-possessed gold should make up the portion of your overall holdings that is for long-term maintaining. Gold is a store of value, not a great investment. It provides no income stream. Buying gold from a dealer and later selling it back to the dealer will carry transaction fees and involve shipping.

Any portion of your holdings that will need to be spent on consumption or investment in the near future should not be held in gold. While GoldMoney does provide a method of transacting, it requires the other party to also have an account with GoldMoney. This makes it impractical for a primary account. Neither your corner store nor your mortgage lender are accepting GoldMoney payments[8] at this point, so having a bank account and debit card continue to be highly practical and convenient.

But this doesn't mean your bank account must be denominated in U.S. dollars. The alternative is foreign currencies. Don't confuse foreign currencies with ForEx. While *ForEx* is a high-risk marketplace for placing bets on the movements of currencies, *foreign currencies* are just like dollars that the central bank of another country is printing up.

Today, all developed countries use fiat currency. Most of these countries are printing money to some degree or another, but several countries have money supplies much more stable than ours in the United States.

The amount of your holdings that you plan on spending on consumption or investment in the near future should be held in a bank account for its convenience. You will do a much better job of maintaining your MPC balance if this bank account is denominated in a currency other than the U.S. dollar. But don't go down to your local bank or a local branch of one of the gigantic, bleeding, bailout-receiving zombie banks—they won't help you buck the dollar. You'll need to go elsewhere.

Before you decide at which bank you will open your account, you must decide what currency you want to hold.

---

[8] To clarify, I encourage you to consider using GoldMoney for holding a portion of your savings, but not for holding the vast majority.

The economic conditions of countries and governments are changing so rapidly that this part of the book is not meant to be timeless. At the time of writing, there are a few countries whose currencies are showing remarkable stability relative to the dollar. One such country is Canada. It's a natural resources country. It's a net exporter of energy, and has the world's second largest oil reserves behind Saudi Arabia.

That could change not too far down the road. Remember when your mother told you, "Don't you hang around with the wrong crowd"? Well, Canada is geographically forced to hang around with the dubiously governed United States—the bully of the world's playground. Having the world's reserve currency[9] is like stealing other countries' lunch money each morning. Our bully reputation is only intensifying, as we've been unable to say "we're sorry" for invading countries for no legitimate reason and, knowingly or unknowingly, expanding an empire.

Suffice it to say that which country holds the top spot for monetary stability will fluctuate. It used to be Switzerland, a pillar of financial stability. The Swiss Franc was one of the last major currencies to sever its link to gold, a recent move that took place on May 1, 2000. Since then, the Swiss have joined the currency-printing party with enthusiasm. Today, Canada holds the crown for monetary stability.

---

[9] The reserve currency is held in significant quantities by many governments. It is also the international pricing currency for products traded on a global market, such as gold and oil. With the dollar as the global reserve currency, the Fed's inflation is spread among the whole world of dollar holders, and thus the value-declining effects of monetary debasement are not borne by the citizens and government of the United States alone.

How To Own Other Currencies

Having a Canadian bank account is a tricky affair. As our geographic neighbor, their hanging around the U.S. government has led them to pass their own version of the Patriot Act.[10] As a result, opening an account at a Canadian bank absolutely requires an in-person visit to a bank branch. You can't appoint another person to open the account for you, even with a written and notarized limited power-of-attorney.[11] While inconvenient, I strongly urge you to consider visiting Canada for the purpose of opening a bank account.

An alternative to opening an account with a Canadian bank is to open one with a non-Canadian bank that offers accounts in Canadian dollars. At the time of writing, one convenient option is an account in Belize.

At this point it is useful to clear up a potential confusion. When we hear of "offshore banking", it is often a matter of *hiding* assets, possibly for tax evasion. I'm not advocating hiding assets or evading taxes. I know nothing about either

---

[10] The Patriot Act is an incredible atrocity and an assault on our basic freedoms. It is unconstitutional on a number of grounds. A several-hundred-page document, it was made available to members of Congress for voting about 15 minutes before they were to vote for or against it. In other words, Congress was forced to vote on a law that was impossible for them to read and review within the time allotted.

[11] A limited power-of-attorney is a document in which one party grants another party authority to act on his behalf for a limited purpose or a limited amount of time. These instruments are often used for the execution of a single transaction, such as a real estate closing or the opening of a bank account.

topic. Instead, I advocate offshore banking for the purpose of maintaining the value of your holdings, and reducing your exposure to the fragile and unhealthy system of financial institutions in the United States.[12]

Some large banks in Belize offer a menu of over 15 currencies to hold in your bank account. You don't have to travel there, as an appointee can open an account for you. This will inevitably involve a fee, but when measured properly in MPC, this fee will be dwarfed by the amount of savings you will keep by exiting the dollar. In other words, paying the fee and exiting the dollar will put you in a net positive position. *To find additional resources for opening foreign bank accounts, visit FiveStepsToFreedomBook.com.*

More reasons to exit the dollar

Taking an honest inventory of the operation of our government today can only result in disgust. A trillion dollar deficit. Tens of trillions in unfunded welfare liabilities. Laws passed without being read. The loyalty of most politicians is to the lobbyists and special interest groups who pad their pockets, fund their campaigns, and make their careers possible.

---

[12] As one small example of the weakness of financial institutions in the U.S., consider the "bank stress tests" the government conducted on the banks that received bailout funds from the Troubled Asset Relief Program. The tests reported that banks needed over $75 billion to reach a 25-to-1 debt-to-equity ratio.

What do we truly have to vote for? The press exercises an incredible amount of control over the outcome of voting. At one point in the 2008 Presidential campaign, candidate Ron Paul had received more campaign contributions from *individuals* than any other Republican candidate. Yet, during the South Carolina Republican debate, journalist Carl Cameron asked, "Congressman Paul, yet another question about electability. Do you have any, sir?"

We do have one way to vote, and that's our choice of whether or not to hold the dollar. The government is on a runaway path of exponential growth in size and spending, with little or no real sign of public benefit.[13] This is possible only through our fiat currency, provided by the Fed.

Owning dollars has a multiplier effect in supporting the system that increases the abusive powers of big corporations and big government. Depositing 100 dollars into a bank gives that bank the right to lend about 90 dollars to someone else, while still showing the original dollars as part of your balance. More often than not, the loaned 90 dollars will end up as another bank deposit. From it, about 81 dollars will be further lent. This process can continue on to multiple levels to create approximately 1,000 dollars—all based on your original 100 dollars. The chief beneficiary in this scheme is the banking system that earns interest on the money that was created at the very moment they lent it.

---

[13] Nearly all theories of government program success can be proven faulty by reading Henry Hazlitt's *Economics in One Lesson*. It's an easy read and if you've made it this far in my book you owe it to yourself to breeze through Hazlitt's classic piece on the basics of Austrian economic thought.

Holding dollars in a bank account serves to put more people in debt to banks, and to put more suspiciously-earned interest in the hands of banks. Loans are not a source of wealth—productivity is. Remember that money has no use in and of itself. It can only be used as a medium of exchange. The things it is exchanged for—goods for consumption as well as resources[14]—are the true valuables. A bank creating money out of thin air to make a loan does nothing to *create* resources. While it gives the borrower the ability to obtain resources, that ability is diverted away from all others who hold dollars. This is because their dollars then have a smaller claim on the available resources as a result of the loan adding to the total money supply.

> *Permit me to issue and control the money of*
> *the nation and I care not who makes its laws.*
> *- Mayer Amschel Rothschild, 18th Century*

Over 200 hundred years ago, Rothschild understood that a privately owned and operated central banking system held more power than even lawmakers. So many of us today feel we are helpless in the matter of stamping out corruption. Alas, an epiphany—we are financing this corruption! Our choice to hold much of our savings in dollars is a vote in favor of the very system that bleeds us.

---

[14] Resources can be equipment, labor, ideas, etc.

Isn't it unpatriotic to dump dollars?

The idea that dumping dollars causes harm to our country is ludicrous. It is harmful alright—but to the culprits of our financial slavery. The effect on the nation as a whole is incredibly positive. Remember, our real value as a nation is our resources: our labor, innovation, ingenuity, equipment, technology, land, etc.

No matter what happens to our money supply, our resources are our resources. And delivering a crushing blow to the banking system that is bullying the world will likely improve our ability to use our resources more efficiently. Less manipulation would mean fewer false signals, such as the artificially low interest rates that invited the housing bubble.

In fact, I contend that it is unpatriotic to *not* dump dollars.

Every person you meet is harmed to some degree by the undeserved, secret power exercised by our monetary manipulators. Every dollar that you deposit into a bank is oppressing your fellow citizens—of the U.S. and of the world—through inflation and economic instability.

Twenty years ago, using a nearby bank was a convenience second to none. Today, with Internet banking technology, there is no excuse for using the bank across the street exclusively. Sure, own a domestic bank account. But if you want to vote down the growing fascism in our country, use that dollar-based bank account as little as possible. The debit card tied to a foreign bank account will work almost anywhere, just like a domestic debit card.

Don't worry about currency conversions. No matter what currency your foreign bank account holds, your debit card transactions will be automatically converted to the local currency. If you are buying lunch in the U.S., your card will pay in U.S. dollars. You won't be exposed to the U.S. dollar because your bank will only convert to dollars at the very moment the debit card transaction is initiated. Similarly, going to an ATM will instantly convert your withdrawal to local currency and dispense it to you as such.

Retirement Accounts

The average American has a significant amount of their total holdings in an IRA and/or 401(k) account. Therefore, in practice every step of the 5 Steps To Freedom is designed to also be executed in any retirement accounts you have. Although not advertised by Wall Street brokerages, IRA and 401(k) plans can be restructured to pull most or all of their assets out of the stock market and even put them into precious metals and foreign bank accounts.

Let's revisit the plan for maintaining what you have. There are several options. Physical gold is the longest-standing store of value known to man. It has been in use for thousands of years and its stable supply enables you to enact your own gold standard. If you choose to own gold stored in a remote storage facility, an offshore venue is preferred. Owning silver can also be a good supplement and create diversification.

Additionally, an offshore bank account (with a world-wide debit card) is the best way to hold spendable non-dollar currency. Canadian dollars currently show signs of stability, but that could change in the future.

Once you've begun maintaining the value of your holdings, preparing your MPC balance sheet will show you how much you are *not* losing as a result of following the 5 Steps To Freedom. If that has you excited, your enthusiasm, along with your future wealth, will be stoked by the exponential power of what comes next.

STEP 4: MULTIPLY

CHAPTER TEN

THE MAGIC MULTIPLIER

1. Go to work to make money
2. Spend less than your earn
3. Save and/or invest the remainder of your earnings
    for your future

Item 2 of the standard life plan is financial logic in its most basic form. Item 1 of the life plan, for some, is a magnificent affair. There are people who are innovating and changing the world.

Everyone else is selling time.

There is nothing wrong with selling time—working for a salary or hourly wage. Commissioned salespeople are also selling time, albeit at a pay rate that they have some control over. For those of us selling time, it is Item 3 of the life plan that has the secret ingredient to accelerate freedom. It is so potent that what you are about to read may remind you of the absurd claims of a TV infomercial. However, don't confuse amazing with absurd. Pause the doubt and fear sections of your brain long enough to fathom the power of wealth multiplication as we cover a few examples...

Joe1 makes $35 per hour, or $6,066 per month. He is able to save $2,000 per month (or $2 MPC) and is following the first 3 steps of the 5 steps to freedom—measure, move, and maintain. Measured in MPC he is maintaining the value of his savings. He lives modestly on about $2,500 per month (or $2.50 MPC) and the rest goes to income taxes.

After 20 years Joe1 has amassed $480 MPC, mostly held in gold. If he wanted to retire and continue his modest lifestyle, he would only be able to fund 16 more years at $2.50 MPC per month. So he has to keep working instead. After Year 30, he has amassed $720 MPC. At that point, he could afford to retire with 24 years of expenses at his current modest spending level. He has done much better than those who follow the conventional financial plan that involves masking a long-term systematic loss of wealth due to monetary manipulation.

Cut Your Working Years By 43%

Joe2 is just like Joe1, except he has included the 4th step to freedom—*multiplying* his holdings through buying investments. Remember, Joe1 had to work for 30 years and spend meagerly to save enough wealth to retire with the same meager lifestyle. Joe2's earnings, spending, and savings are identical. But after only 17 years, Joe2's path diverges from Joe1's. He's amassed $408 MPC and decides to buy an investment. As you learn in the coming pages, the best investments are those that produce income. Joe2 uses his $408 MPC to buy an investment that pays $40.80 MPC of income per year. This investment provides a basic 10% income-based return-on-investment ("ROI") which, as you will see later, is very achievable. This income amounts to $3.40 MPC per month or an after-tax income of $2.55 MPC per month. His investment has replaced his income!

He has discovered something important—**not only can *he* work for an income, but *his wealth* can work for an income too**. Now he can do whatever he wants with his time. Maybe he'll continue working, but now he can choose to do something he <u>truly enjoys</u> even if it doesn't pay well. Or maybe he'll never work another day in his life. It's up to him. In 17 years he's achieved what took Joe1 30 years to achieve. *Joe2 cut his working years by 43%.* In fact, it's much more than Joe1 achieved. Joe1's 24 years of retirement was paid for by *spending his savings*. After 24 years of retirement Joe1 would have $0 MPC left over.

Joe2, on the other hand, is not spending savings—he's *spending the income* he receives from his investment. After 24 years, he still owns the investment that his $408 bought, in addition to enjoying an amount of income that replaces his wages. And this is the fruit of one single decision to buy one single investment.

Cut Your Working Years
By ANOTHER 41%

The real power of multiplication comes into play with Joe3. His earnings and spending are the same, but he doesn't wait 17 years to buy an investment. He starts buying investments with his savings at the end of the first year, and continues to use his savings to buy another investment each year thereafter. Just as with Joe2, Joe3 is buying investments that produce an income-based 10 percent ROI. There's something amazing to point out here. Each year Joe3 is buying a new investment, using his unspent work income from that year *and* his investment income from that year. This means that each year he is buying a larger investment that produces larger income, thus leading to an even larger investment purchase the following year, which leads to an even larger increase in income, and so on and so forth. This is known as *compounding*. Some claim that Albert Einstein called compounding the eighth wonder of the world.

In the case of Joe3, after only 10 years he has amassed $425.93 MPC worth of investments that are paying him $42.59 MPC per year in income. That's $3.54 MPC per month, or about $2.66 MPC after taxes. He has reached the same retirement point as Joe2, but in only 10 years! Joe3 worked 41 percent less than Joe2 and 66 percent less than Joe1. Because the power of multiplication is working hard for him, he doesn't have to work as long.

Cut Your Work Week by 27%

Here's another way to look at it. If he does work as **long** as Joe2, he doesn't have to work as **much**. Joe2 worked 40 hours per week for 17 years to build investment holdings of about $400 MPC. With the power of investment multiplication, Joe3 could amass $400 MPC of investment holdings in 17 years, which requires saving only $0.75 MPC per month. This means Joe3 could work only 29 hours per week instead of 40.

Increase Your Spending By 50%

Consider another way to look at it. Joe3, harnessing the power of investment multiplication, could **spend** much more than Joe2 during his working years. He wouldn't have to keep to such a frugal lifestyle. Again, if he works full time for 17 years to amass $400 MPC of investment holdings, he only needs to save $0.75 MPC per month. This means he could increase his monthly spending by 50 percent and still reach the same retirement lifestyle as Joe2 after 17 years.

Increase Your Income
By 848% Without A Job

And yet another way to look at it. Joe3 could keep the frugal spending, work for 30 years and enjoy an extraordinarily lavish lifestyle in retirement. At the end of a 30-year career, Joe3 would have amassed $6,186 MPC. At that point his *automatic investment income* would be $618 MPC per year or $51.55 MPC per month before taxes. That's 848% higher than his original full time working income and requires no work!

CHAPTER ELEVEN

THE SLAVE BECOMES THE MASTER

Now you must ask yourself an important question.

*Am I willing to learn about real investing if it could
cut my working years by 66 percent, increase my spending
by 50 percent, or increase my income by 848 percent?*

Conventional thought says that investing is complicated, boring, and difficult. The solution for the masses is mutual funds, index funds, and exchange-traded funds. Yet you know from earlier chapters these all lead to a true loss of value in your holdings.

The first 3 steps in the 5 steps to freedom—**measure, move,** and **maintain**—are unbelievably simple and easy. The fourth step is to *multiply* your holdings. The rate of multiplication is up to you. If you want to do absolutely nothing, you can choose to multiply your MPC holdings by 1 and not buy any income-producing investments. It's your choice and that would be completely acceptable.

But the idea that investing outside of the stock market is complicated, boring, and difficult is just plain wrong. I spend most of my days interacting with the growing legions of people who have decided to become real investors. These are people who believe the stakes are too high to walk away from investing. Selling your time for decades just isn't necessary.

These real investors aren't number whizzes. Most of them lead very exciting lives. Some of their investment activity is exciting in and of itself, and what they choose to do with their increased wealth and time is even more exciting.

Ten years ago the topics of investing, economics, politics, and law weren't the least bit appealing to me. Since then I've realized that getting to the heart of the matter—how learning about these topics will give me the lifestyle and freedoms I desire—has torn through the illusion that I'm not interested in investing. I was previously told that investing was all about price-to-earnings ratios, spreads, microscopic arbitrage, moving averages, technical analysis, and that I would need to be glued to a computer screen with a scientific calculator in hand during trading hours. I wasn't interested in that at all.

As it turns out, "that" isn't investing. "That," along with blindly dumping money into huge investment funds, is the commercially advertised version of investing.

The version of investing I am now happy to unfold before you has nothing to do with huge financial institutions lined up on a single street on the tiny island of Manhattan. It has everything to do with yanking your wealth out of those slick-suited clowns' hands and doing things that make sense.

You see, there is a world of investment opportunities out there everywhere you look. But what we've been told is that investment opportunities for the average person are only accessible through Wall Street. These blinders are worn by almost every American investor. It's time we take off the blinders and put on reality goggles to reveal the untold truth: Not a single opportunity is born on Wall Street. Only repackaged investment opportunities that originated in the real world can appear on Wall Street in the form of a stock or fancy financial instrument, to be included in mutual funds, index funds, and exchange traded funds.

Wall Street operates using the theory of big. It takes something of value, such as a profitable business, and injects financial steroids into it, in order to try to mutate that value into enormous proportions, and this game is played with *your* Individual Retirement Account (IRA) and 401(k) funds. This theory of big has disproven itself right before our eyes. The largest bank failure in American history (Washington Mutual, WaMu) took place in October 2008. The largest insurance failure in American history (American International Group, AIG) has been repeatedly taking place. The largest American car manufacturers can't figure out how to make cars and sell them at a profit anymore. Apparently, bigger isn't always better in the world of finance and business.

What happens when an athlete takes a lot of steroids? Believe it or not, if it's a man, shrunken testicles and the growth of breasts will eventually ensue. In other words, lowered levels of male hormones and increased levels of female hormones—the *opposite* of what the male athlete wanted. The same thing is occurring on Wall Street; the people whose money is in the game for the sake of profit are ultimately experiencing a loss. Today it comes in the form of *reported* losses and tomorrow it will be in the form of *unreported* inflationary losses.

That is what happens when we all, like sheep, follow each other into buying repackaged investment opportunities, rather than finding the real assets ourselves. Outside of the fraudulent game orchestrated on a tiny island in New York, there are plenty of entrepreneurs who create opportunities more along the lines of the theory of *small*. These opportunities aren't advertised on the Internet or TV, and their actual creators share them privately only with people they like. We're loosening the blinders, and by the end of this section you'll be able to fully see the world of real, un-packaged, not-tampered-with investment opportunities.

A Fork In The Road

It's early and quiet. Opening his front door to face a nearly perfect morning, Jacob makes his way across his front lawn toward the mailbox. Lately this mailbox seems to hold the power to either permit passage into a normal day or crush him. Across the street, Phil is still sleeping soundly.

Phil and Jacob both have several things in common. They both like football and Italian food. Both are proud of their sons and never miss the sports games they play in. Most of all they are both concerned about the economic crisis and how it is

---

affecting their financial situation. But they each are reacting to that concern in different ways.

Jacob is frozen in fear and uncertainty. He carefully listens as countless advisors carry on about the importance of staying in the stock market, as it is "poised for a huge rebound". He doesn't recognize how these same advisors failed to tell him to get out before the crash or even in the middle of it… or *ever*, come to think of it.

Phil is fed up. He's an independent thinker, and he doesn't want his family to be dragged down by the misbehavior of Fortune 500 CEOs, Wall Street executives, bankers, and incompetent politicians. He's recently met several people, ranging from moderately to immensely wealthy, who don't use the stock market as their main investment. He doesn't consider this a coincidence, and has set out to learn from these people.

Jacob tries not to think about how stuffing cash under a mattress has outperformed the stock market over the past ten years, the same way that an overweight person tries to ignore the lumpy figure in the mirror.

Phil is building real estate holdings and profiting *when he buys* using methods he learned from his wealthy mentors.

Jacob is cringing when he pulls his 401(k) statement out of his mailbox. He can avoid viewing his e-statements online, but he can't neglect his mailbox. He's tired of seeing it go up 4 percent for every 15 percent it goes down. He has a sick feeling of guilt that he is somehow failing his wife and kids.

Phil is learning about how money is created

and regulated and is finding ways to profit from the Fed's printing presses running in high gear.

Jacob just wishes he could stop losing money.

Phil stopped losing money and has replaced his old portfolio of empty hopes with an understandable portfolio of solid investments.

Jacob doesn't have to worry about paying taxes on his investments because they are losing money.

Phil also doesn't have to worry about paying taxes on his investments, but it is because he is using special IRA & 401(k) accounts to get tax-favored status on his alternative investment profits.

The primary difference between the two is that Jacob is just waiting for his financial situation, against all odds, to work itself out... while Phil is *doing something* about his situation. Phil knows that knowledge is power, and he is in constant pursuit of knowledge that will help him make smart financial decisions that are geared to benefit him and his family.

After meeting Jacob, Phil, and many others, I've dedicated myself to helping you pursue knowledge that can replace your financial worries and fears. Worrying is the result of not having enough knowledge and control to get where you want to go. If doing what's popular (financially) feels like being in a taxi cab driven by an aggressive maniac who doesn't speak your language, then putting the knowledge in this section to work for you is like being in the *driver's seat* of your dream car. You face a fork in the road where you can follow either Jacob or Phil.

Some people call what we're going to cover "alternative assets." It's ironic that we now have to use the term "alternative assets" to describe anything that isn't packaged and sold by Wall Street firms. Just 50 years ago the stock market was an alternative that nobody in his right mind felt comfortable investing his retirement funds in.[15] A few decades of financial wizardry, paired with amazing marketing, and now we must refer to direct ownership of real assets as "the alternative". The lessons herein will show you how to double your wealth as often as you like. There's something known as the *Rule of 72*. This rule makes it easy to estimate the *compounding* we examined earlier.

Simply divide 72 by your average annualized return on investment ("ROI"), and you get the approximate number of years it will take to double your money. A 10 percent return means you'll double your money every 7.2 years. You can do even better than that if you so desire. Not only is this achievable—it's easier than you may think.

What you actually do with this information is up to you. Without an excessive amount of hard work you can average a 10 percent ROI. With a substantial amount of hard work you can average a 20 percent ROI. Some of the investment stories in the coming pages involve ROIs of several hundred percent on a single deal, and not based on luck. Clear your mental slate to make room.

---

[15] According to the Survey of Financial Characteristics of Consumers, in 1962 only 18 percent of American households owned stock.

ROI and Years Needed to Double Wealth	
Average ROI	**Double Wealth Every…**
10%	7.2 years
12%	6 years
15%	4.8 years
18%	4 years
20%	3.6 years

A Faulty Theory

Dumping the faulty theory that Wall Street's stock market is a magic money machine that "always produces 8 percent returns over the long run" leads to a better way.

The good news is: You can use your retirement funds to directly purchase real assets. Your stock market portfolio can be converted to a portfolio of real and diversified assets rather than worthless pieces of digital paper controlled by large corrupt institutions. Even if your wealth is tied up in an IRA, 401(k) or similar retirement account, you can directly convert some or all of that account to own real assets with no middleman. And you can do all this without triggering taxes or penalties. This is often referred to as a "self-directed" IRA, IRA LLC, or Solo 401(k).

This is an extremely popular yet confusing topic riddled with misinformation, but I've done all the hard work for you in identifying and integrating just about all the accurate information there is. Because there is so much wealth (over $10 trillion) stashed away in retirement accounts, and because so many Americans have them (over 100 million), most of the case studies that follow involve self-directed IRA or 401(k) plans.

We'll be covering over a dozen real-life case studies. Here's a sneak peek…

- One man who turned $34,000 into $2.6 million by buying and creating private mortgage notes

- Two frustrated and tired foreclosure flippers who changed their direction and bought $13 million worth of real estate for $6 million in less than two years

- An airline pilot whose global perspective led him to earning a passive 48 percent return from real estate construction in a country that is among the world's healthiest economies despite the global meltdown

- A couple in a rural town who turned $300,000 into $900,000 by buying real estate for its mineral rights

- A young entrepreneur who used his Rolodex and understanding of early-stage startups to create a portfolio of small business investments that inspires more confidence than any position he had ever held in the publicly traded stock market

And equally, if not more important, we'll examine case studies of people who lost wealth because they made the most common mistakes, and we'll look at the best ways for you to avoid these mistakes. Get ready: here come the good, bad, and the ugly. These lessons cost millions of dollars to those who lived them, and you get the inside scoop...

CASE STUDY:
Buying Controlling Interest in a Community

"Imagination is more important than knowledge."
- Albert Einstein

Lenny and Mason had been working hard for years flipping foreclosure properties and making a little profit. They promoted their business with signs reading, "We buy homes! Call us today." The profit was good but not great. The buying of foreclosures and short-sale properties may have provided the pair with an income, but they were working furiously, exhausting themselves rehabbing properties all over South Carolina. They'd fix one up and sell it and then look for their next deal—sometimes driving dozens of miles back and forth between their various properties and sitting in traffic for hours.

Both Lenny and Mason were ready for a change in strategy. At the time, the real estate bubble had blown condo prices so out of proportion that apartments could be converted to condo units for individual sale at a handsome profit. Living and working in Myrtle Beach, they took this condo conversion idea to larger cities in the region. When they identified one promising property in Atlanta, they jumped in the car and headed off to investigate further.

Once they got there, Lenny and Mason had an epiphany. The solid economy of Atlanta was far more promising for sound investment strategies than the fragile, bubble-dependent tourist economy of Myrtle Beach. Everything they saw suggested that Atlanta was a healthy and vibrant city with plenty of opportunities for investment.

> The 1996 Olympics prompted rapid growth in Atlanta, and in recent years it has been the fastest-growing metropolitan area in the country—between 2000 and 2006, the city added more than 890,000 new residents.

They soon learned from real estate agents about a major transportation development system being planned for the downtown Atlanta area. The city was converting the old railroad tracks that ran around the edge of the downtown area into a light-rail system that would put 25 percent of Atlanta's population within walking distance of the new transportation system. A network of public parks and multi-use trails would supplement the 22-mile loop of transit development along the historic railroad corridor that circled downtown and connected many neighborhoods.

> **Key Features of the planned Beltline:**
> - Nearly 1,300 acres of new green space and parks
> - 33 miles of multi-use trails
> - A 22-mile loop of transit connecting dozens of neighborhoods
> - Approximately 30,000 new jobs in 20 economic development areas
> - 5,600+ affordable workforce housing units
> - Touches and connects 45 neighborhoods
> - Investments in pedestrian access, streetscapes, public art, historic preservation, and environmental cleanup

Tired of turning piecemeal deal after deal to grind out an adequate profit, Lenny and Mason explored the opportunity to invest in homes around the Atlanta downtown area, which they believed could only increase in value as the Beltline project unfolded. But the land and properties were more expensive than the partners could afford with their personal savings. So they decided to use money sitting dormant in their old employers' 401(k) accounts to fund their projects through their newly formed Urban Real Estate Redevelopment Group LLC.

Urban Real Estate Redevelopment Group LLC was owned by Lenny Enterprises LLC (owned wholly by Lenny) and Mason Enterprises LLC (owned wholly by Mason). *See the illustration below.*

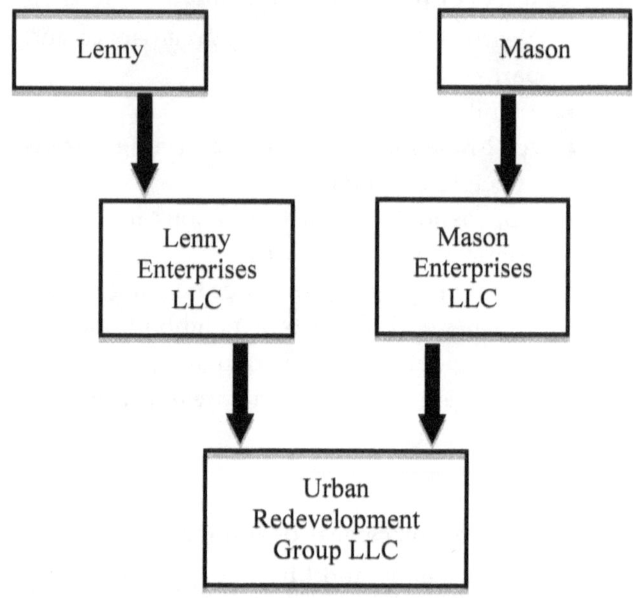

As entrepreneurs, they had already set up Solo 401(k) plans and funded them with rollovers from pre-existing retirement plans. **Lenny Enterprises LLC** adopted **Lenny Enterprises Solo 401(k) Plan** and **Mason Enterprises LLC** adopted **Mason Enterprises Solo 401(k) Plan**. Using a financial strategy that is unique to the Solo 401(k), Lenny and Mason could each borrow up to 50 percent of the value of their account or $50,000 (whichever was less) for anything they wanted. So they each took out $50,000 tax-free and contributed it as startup capital to their partnership, **Urban Redevelopment Group LLC**. They would each repay their loans to their Solo 401(k) at an interest rate of 1 percent over prime, amortized over five years. This strategy gave them a total of $100,000 to invest in real estate without triggering any taxes or distributions.

The pair sat down with a couple of friends and advisors in brainstorming sessions for putting together their Atlanta real estate plan. They wanted to take a different approach from the strategies that were promoted in all the bubble-oriented house-flipping books they had read. The strategy they devised was to focus on acquiring properties close together in a neighborhood that had room for improvement. They knew that if they purchased several properties in a single neighborhood and fixed them up, they could have some control over the pricing of the homes in that neighborhood. They also knew that homes near the Beltline project would have growing demand as the development progressed.

Lenny and Mason used several Internet research tools to find information about the development and revitalization opportunities, including available properties, zoning and land use maps, demographics, development potential, and incentives for each of the nine corridors: Cascade Road, Campbellton Road, Donald Lee Hollowell Parkway, Jonesboro Road, Memorial Drive, Metropolitan Parkway, ML King Jr. Drive, Simpson Road, and the Turner Field Stadium Area.

A study by the Local Government Commission (LGC) reported that, "Residential and commercial projects near transit typically appreciate in value more rapidly than other projects. As demand for scarce properties near transit stops increases, this trend will continue".

For Lenny and Mason this meant a chance to realize healthy profits if they could find the right neighborhood on which to focus their acquisition and rehab efforts. The two discovered a community that many investors had overlooked because of its crime-ridden streets, and junky, vacant homes. This was the first "ah-ha!" moment for these investors. Gasoline prices were on the rise, causing a trend of people moving out of the suburbs and back into cities so they would need to drive less or not at all. Lenny and Mason studied the adjacent neighborhoods and found that this particular community was sandwiched between a more-affluent community and a more poverty-stricken one. It was close to the new light-rail system and not far from the Georgia Dome, where major sports events took place. They thought this community would be an ideal match for their strategy.

So, the two invested in their first property, putting $10,000 down on a $50,000 home. They made a list of remodeling improvements that would cost about $30,000 and hired an appraiser to estimate the projected value after the improvements. The appraisal came in at $180,000! This was the second "ah-ha!" moment they shared, because they knew they had uncovered a profitable strategy that could be repeated. They made the improvements and refinanced the mortgage loan from $40,000 to $135,000. The bank was happy with this because the loan-to-value ratio was still only 75 percent—a relatively low-risk loan. At the closing of the refinance, Lenny and Mason walked away with more than $90,000 cash to fund future property acquisitions and rehabbing projects.

As the pair purchased each property, they helped raise the value of the neighborhood. They put unemployed people on the streets to work rehabbing the properties. The community supported Lenny and Mason because they truly wanted to improve the neighborhood. They joined forces with nonprofit groups to create after-school programs that would keep once-troublesome teens constructively busy. They created attractions such as community art walks. House by house, they began turning a once-dying neighborhood into a promising one. The police patrolled more frequently, crime dropped, cooperation grew, and the neighborhood gradually became more attractive for people looking to be close to downtown but still live in an affordable community.

Their strategy was to raise the value of the neighborhood by making improvements and having a controlling interest in the community. Real estate values are set by buyers and sellers, and as long as the pair controlled the greatest number of homes in an area, they could have a substantial influence over home prices.

As the housing bubble began to burst, Lenny and Mason continued purchasing homes in the same neighborhood, but for even lower prices! They walked away from real estate auctions with 10 properties at a time, purchased for prices as low as $17,000. They executed their plan well. Their concept is similar to an investor buying a controlling interest in a publicly-traded company so that he can make changes to the company—only Lenny and Mason were doing it with tens of thousands of dollars instead of billions. The two partners were determined to have a controlling interest in the neighborhood so that they could transform it from a ghetto to a vibrant community.

In just two years, they purchased 120 homes by buying, remodeling, pulling equity out through refinancing, and repeating the process. Each property was purchased at a huge bargain.[16] Their initial goal was to resell the properties. They own $13 million worth of properties and have only $6 million in debt. But as they progressed, it became clear that holding onto the properties created remarkable cash flow. Today they have rented out about 50 properties, and are continuing to rent additional properties as improvements are completed. Once they rent out 100 properties, they will have over $50,000 in profits per month.

Lenny and Mason enjoy a good living while they continue to improve a community that had been pleading for creative investors to take an interest in it. The pair continue to operate their real estate investing out of their LLC, and with their wives' help, they each contribute over $100,000 per year to their Solo 401(k) plans—the investment vehicles that provided them the startup capital they used to grow $7 million of real estate equity in just two years.

---

[16] For each property, the "subject-to improvements" estimated value was much higher than the sum of acquisition and improvement costs.

Balance Sheet July 2006 – Urban Redevelopment Group LLC					
Assets	USD	MPC	Liabilities	USD	MPC
Cash	100,000	100.00			
Total Assets	100,000	100.00	Total Liabilities	0	0.00
Net Worth	100,000	100.00	(MPC conversion rate: 1,000)		

Balance Sheet January 2009 – Urban Redevelopment Group LLC					
Assets	USD	MPC	Liabilities	USD	MPC
Properties	13,000,000	10,612.24	Mortgages	6,000,000	4,897.96
Total Assets	13,000,000	10,612.24	Total Liabilities	6,000,000	4,897.96
Net Worth	7,000,000	5,714.29			
Previous Net Worth	100,000	100.00			
Net Worth Change	+6,900,000	+5,614.29	*(MPC conversion rate: 1,225)*		
Net Worth Change %	+6900%	+5614%			

What made their project so successful was their focus on making a positive impact on the community. When Mason first toured the neighborhood, he had a vision of how it would look once they had redeveloped it into a safe and thriving community like the one adjacent to it. As the ultimate people-person, Lenny stepped in to coordinate between homeowners, residents, bankers, contractors, public officials, and others to bring that vision to life. Where other investors saw shady, dangerous characters roaming the streets of this neighborhood at all hours, Lenny and Mason saw people desperate to not be ignored.

I recently accompanied Lenny for a couple days as he managed their "on the street" operations, while Mason managed the other aspects from Myrtle Beach. As Lenny drove through the neighborhood streets in his minivan, proudly marked "Urban Real Estate Redevelopment Group LLC," residents waved in excitement and sincere appreciation for the transformation in progress. Some residents who had lived there for more than 20 years had watched the community take a turn for the worse. Lenny and Mason arrived not a moment too soon to restore their community. For themselves, the investment partners made a move that can serve either as a means to early retirement or as a fantastic launch pad for further wealth-building projects.

CASE STUDY:
Pre-Construction Popularity

*"Whenever you find that you are on the
side of the majority, it is time to reform."*
- Mark Twain

Julie had never invested in real estate because she didn't know where to start. By 2005, so many of her friends had been cashing in on the real estate boom that it seemed like it didn't matter where she started—*just buy real estate*. She didn't have much savings, and her $50,000 IRA was her only source of funds. She wanted to make as much money as possible. The best way to do that was to get in early, her real estate agent, Donna, told her. Donna had helped dozens of others collectively make millions of dollars in the past few years, and she was excited to be doing the same for Julie.

Donna was aiming Julie's sights on pre-construction opportunities. The price of real estate was going up so consistently and so rapidly that the earlier you tied up a property, the better. In fact, new condo buildings took preconstruction reservations, and by the time construction was finished, the price of the property was often much higher than the reservation price. What's more, by that time, many of the reservation holders had already "flipped", or sold, their reservation contract to another buyer, she told Julie.

This type of thing was going on so regularly in the waterfront coastal areas that it was thought only a fool could argue with such an investment formula. Julie certainly wasn't a fool. So she picked out a development project in the class of real estate that was appreciating most: luxury condominiums. At a price tag of $500,000, needing only a five percent down payment to reserve one, Julie reserved two, using the entire $50,000 in her self-directed IRA. Because her IRA custodian was "passive," the custodian just followed her directions without a word about the investment being said.

The oh-so-familiar dollar signs shone in her eyes. If these $500,000 units became worth $700,000 within eight months, Julie's reservation contracts would be worth $225,000 each. Two of those would equal eight years' worth of Julie's employment earnings. Why, she could even quit her job and just reserve luxury condos for a living. What was she doing working, anyway?

You know what came next. The real estate boom turned into a real estate bust a bit too soon for Julie. Lenders and buyers sobered up just in time for no one to be around for Julie to flip her reservation contract to. She didn't have the funds to buy the properties, so she lost her entire $50,000.

Balance Sheet June 2006					
Assets	**USD**	**MPC**	**Liabilities**	**USD**	**MPC**
IRA	50,000	50.00	Credit card debt	4,500	4.50
Savings account	2,500.00	2.50			
Total Assets	52,500	52.50	Total Liabilities	4,500	4.50
Net Worth	48,000	48.00	*(MPC conversion rate: 1,000)*		

Balance Sheet May 2007					
Assets	**USD**	**MPC**	**Liabilities**	**USD**	**MPC**
IRA	0	0.00	Credit card debt	4,000	3.77
Savings account	2,000	1.89			
Total Assets	2,000	1.89	Total Liabilities	4,000	3.77
Net Worth	-2,000	-1.89			
Previous Net Worth	48,000	48.00			
Net Worth Change	-50,000	-49.89	*(MPC conversion rate: 1,060)*		
Net Worth Change %	-104.2%	-103.9%			

No one said anything to Julie about her method of investing. Not a word was uttered about her lack of diversification—100 percent of her investable assets were placed in a single real estate project—or her inability to buy even the condos she had reserved. Like many others who reserved condos, she did not want to actually *own* the condos. But she took it a step further and didn't even want to *buy* them. Instead, she expected that just pretending to be a serious buyer for a few months would pay more than eight years of an honest job. Ridiculous thoughts like these offer a pretty good indication of a bubble. Just as shoeshine boys gave stock tips in the boom that preceded the Great Depression, modern-day shoeshine boys were all giving each other real estate investment tips.

The media threw fuel onto the fire by profiling various fast-food workers, waitresses, college students, factory workers, and janitors who had turned into full-time real estate investors. Anyone can do this, magazines and TV shows suggested. Working a regular job is just stupid when you can be paid millions to pretend to want to buy or own real estate that you could never actually afford.

How To See An Investment Bubble

Only a small minority of Americans, around 3 percent to 5 percent, are financially independent. It has always been that way. Consider for a moment what would happen if everybody's bank account balances were quadrupled tomorrow. Would that make us all wealthy? Unfortunately, that wouldn't do anything for anyone. Money in and of itself has no use. Its value derives from the real goods and services for which the money can be traded. If everyone's money quadrupled overnight, there would be no change in the resources or goods or services that money could be traded for. Because everyone else's money also quadrupled, sellers of goods and services would quadruple their prices.

The kind of uniform prosperity promised by a bubble is impossible. Wealth is a matter of your holdings *relative* to others' holdings. Everyone can't be wealthy because everyone isn't going to handle his or her finances exactly the same way. What does this mean in terms of bubbles? If you see an unusually easy way to make money, and a lot of people are (increasingly) doing it…then it's probably a bubble.

The same holds true of the stock market. More and more people are doing it, and it has become a bubble itself. Historically, average people don't buy into the stock market, but today, over two thirds do. Ironically, the same law that brought us the most powerful tax-favored investment vehicles (the 401(k) and IRA) is also partly to blame for the stock market bubble.

As we continue, we will alternate between stories of success and failure with investing outside the stock market. Just as a success story gives you ideas about what to do, it is essential to also study failures to learn what *not* to do.

Plenty of exciting opportunities that don't require you to lose your mind exist all around you. The next case study is a fantastic example.

CASE STUDY:
Real Estate With
A Natural (Gas) Twist

Every day, you can hear on the news about how bad our economy is: unemployment is increasing; foreclosures are skyrocketing; businesses collapse; banks clamor for capital from the government as they try to shore up their financial losses; sneaky, greedy swindlers look for opportunities to prey on people in need; and the government continues to ask Americans to spend their way out of the recession, a strategy that makes no sense at all. Listening to the arguments between optimists and pessimists, Democrats and Republicans, and pundits of all shapes, colors and sizes will usually lead to mental and spiritual surrender.

Or you can switch off the TV, put down the newspaper (if one still exists in your town), and learn from savvy investors like the couple that I am going to introduce to you. Janice and Frank Templeman are real estate brokers and, even in "the worst of times", they have been profiting by practicing what they preach. But they didn't do it the traditional way. They didn't do it by turning their hard-earned money over to someone else who invested it in dubious paper certificates.

Other people recommended that Janice just buy stocks, but Janice knew she wanted to invest in real estate, and she wanted to find a retirement vehicle that would allow her to do that. The laws surrounding retirement investment accounts remain a mystery to many. But those who seek information find amazing opportunities awaiting them. Self-directed investing of their retirement account made a tremendous difference for the Templemans.

"When I found out that I could set up a retirement plan that would allow me to invest in real estate, which is something I know very well, I was excited about that," said Janice.

In 2004, the Templemans set up two self-directed IRAs and began doing small real estate transactions, buying and reselling properties and returning the profit to their IRAs.

> At this point, don't worry too much about understanding how a self-directed retirement plan works—that can be learned later. Just know that IRA and 401(k) funds can be transferred (tax-free) to a specially-structured IRA or 401(k) that will allow the account-holder to make almost any profit-driven transaction.

"We had an opportunity to buy 60 acres of land with our IRAs. But in the process, before we were able to close on it, someone approached us to buy it from us, and we were going to make a pretty good profit on it after only about 20 minutes. We told them we were going to make some money on this transaction and the buyers said, 'We don't care. We want to buy it,'" Janice said.

The deal successfully closed, and with the proceeds from their 60-acre sale now in their IRAs, the couple immediately began looking for their next investment. Each transaction became increasingly more tedious with complications, which we'll discuss later. The couple wanted more investment freedom and the ability to have total self-directed control for their next transaction.

They found a 57-acre property with a house on it. The property was valued at $340,000, which was more than the couple had in cash in their IRAs. So they began looking at options.

During this search, they discovered the Solo 401(k), which included features that went far beyond their self-directed IRAs. With the Solo 401(k), the couple could put away more tax-deferred money each year. They could also complete their real estate transactions without processing them through a third-party custodian, because the Solo 401(k) didn't require them to have one. This meant that they could save money on needless custodial transaction fees and not miss an investment opportunity because of delayed custodial responses. It made sense. So, the couple set up a single Solo 401(k) plan to roll both their IRAs into. Nevertheless, they were still short on funds and unable to purchase the 57 acres alone.

"This particular property had been on the market for about a month. The owner was offering 50 percent of the mineral rights (natural gas) to go along with it," said Janice.

The Templemans' son, an attorney, had advised the couple to look for land with mineral rights because many of his clients had made small fortunes that way. Now, determined to take advantage of this opportunity to buy land and mineral rights, the Templemans contacted a couple of friends and asked if they'd be interested in joining them in the investment. Their goal was to buy 57 acres and then subdivide it for resale in 5- and 10- acre parcels. Their friends, both physicians, agreed. The couple formed **High Sights LLC** to partner their Solo 401(k) funds with their friends' IRA funds to purchase the land.

The plot was originally offered for sale with only 50 percent of the mineral rights. After negotiation, High Sights LLC ended up purchasing the property with 100 percent of the mineral rights for a total purchase price $340,000 ($5,875 per acre). At the time there was no drilling activity on the land, so it was uncertain whether the mineral rights added any real value… until what happened next.

"Shortly after, a big energy company started putting wells in our section. It just so happened that the wells they put in that section were very high-producing wells," said Janice. That means a healthy return. "Since we started getting checks on that, we have received more than $100,000 in 18 months just in royalties off of the natural gas that was extracted."

As you can imagine, this is the kind of investment success story that spreads quickly. Soon buyers came knocking, wanting to purchase the mineral rights.

"All this is still new to our area, but the production in each well drops about 50 percent after the first 18 months and then drops about another 50 percent over the next 18 months," said Frank.

Knowing that, the couples considered selling their rights. By this time the LLC had also purchased a few other properties with mineral rights. The couples also sold much of the LLC's mineral rights.

"We got $8,750 an acre for 57 acres of mineral rights, and we still own the land itself. I thought that first property was just a good piece of ground. We knew the mineral rights could become worth something, but we didn't have a clue they would be that valuable," said Frank.

They received $465,000 from the sale of mineral rights, and the land they still own is valued at an estimated $456,000. After six similar real estate transactions in fewer than two years, the value of the LLC's assets increased from $340,000 to more than $900,000—roughly tripling their initial investment.

The Templemans' investment return was exceptional, but it is not unique for savvy and diligent investors. Janice knew real estate, and she knew how to identify a property that was a good investment. Thanks to their son's knowledge of oil and gas, their strategy to purchase the 57 acres became as much about the mineral rights as the real estate. Mineral rights prices had been rising, and lease values had been increasing in her area, and Janice knew that she could resell the land and improvements alone to at least break even, while still keeping what she was really after—the mineral rights.

Balance Sheet for High Sights LLC – December 2006					
Assets	USD	MPC	Liabilities	USD	MPC
Property	340,000	340.00	Mortgage loan	170,000	170.00
Mineral rights[17]	???	???			
Total Assets	340,000	340.00	Total Liabilities	170,000	170.00
Net Worth	170,000	170.00	(MPC conversion rate: 1,000)		

---

[17] When they purchased the property and its mineral rights, it was unclear what the value of the mineral rights would be. The Templemans saw this as all upside since the price they paid was backed by the value of the property, even without the mineral rights.

Balance Sheet for High Sights LLC– September 2008					
Assets	**USD**	**MPC**	**Liabilities**	**USD**	**MPC**
Properties[18]	850,000	664.06	Mortgage loans	400,000	312.50
Cash	500,000	390.63			
Total Assets	1,350,000	1,054.69	Total Liabilities	400,000	312.50
Net Worth	950,000	742.19			
Previous Net Worth	170,000	170.00			
Net Worth Change	+780,000	+572.19	*(MPC conversion rate: 1,280)*		
Net Worth Change %	+458%	+336%			

---

[18] The previous property had been sold and other properties had been bought and sold at a profit by this point.

Today, the Templemans advise other real estate professionals to do their homework and stay on top of self-directed investment possibilities. "I talk to my friends, and they are absolutely despondent over what is happening to money they thought they had for retirement or college. A lot of people have lost a lot of money in recent months. When I tell them I didn't lose a dime and that I've tripled the value of my Solo 401(k) over the last eighteen months, they want to know how."

Janice Templeman sums it up this way: "If we had not established our self-directed investment accounts, we would not have the cash available for investing that we now have. That's what allows us the ability to act fast with real estate and mineral rights opportunities. It's a lot different from helplessly watching the market, and it has absolutely changed our future."

CASE STUDY:
Pretty Water Equals Ugly Finances

One of the most persistent strategies pursued during the real estate bubble was the drunken pursuit of "pretty water" properties. Let's learn from what can happen when you fall prey to this flawed strategy.

Meet Eric and Alice Fischer. They live in New Jersey but vacation in Florida. They had been visiting that beautiful peninsula since the early 1990s. Year after year, they heard about the continually rising prices of the beach homes they had rented. They started thinking about buying one but weren't too keen on coming up with a large down payment. Then three things happened at about the same time:

1. Home price appreciation in the sunshine state accelerated to a hard-to-resist pace. Many of their friends and family had already bought vacation and investment properties in Florida, and all of them seemed to be locking in annual appreciation that promised a stream of dependable, annual income that could be realized through cash-out refinancing.

2. Ever-so-friendly mortgage lenders had all gotten over that silly 20 percent down-payment requirement, and replaced it with only a 5 percent down-payment requirement. To make it even easier, the loan could be "interest only," resulting in even lower monthly payments.

3. To top things off, they discovered the concept of the self-directed IRA through a custodian company in San Francisco. They learned that Eric's IRA could be rolled over to a special IRA which could buy real estate.

This all added up to such a "no brainer" that Eric and Alice decided to buy two properties instead of only one. The custodian told them they could not live or vacation in the IRA-owned property. Buying two properties meant they could use IRA funds to purchase one property, and buy another one with non-IRA money so that they could make personal use of it. The only problem seemed to be that they didn't start buying their vacation properties earlier.

After being referred to a real estate agent one of their friends used, their property search began, and they mailed the self-directed IRA paperwork off to the custodian in San Francisco. They found a beautiful waterfront home on the intercoastal waterway, just a short drive from the ocean, in a small town called Ormond Beach. It was just a little bit north of their favorite vacation spot, Daytona Beach. With three bedrooms, granite countertops, furniture included, the greenest of green lawns, and a brand new shopping center nearby, the house was perfect. Three streets away, a similar home was for sale with a larger yard but further from the water. Their real estate agent, Rob, told them it was located in a highly desirable area that had been rising in value. With dollar signs in all three sets of eyes, they discussed how all the Northerners were going to be migrating to Florida to live a sunnier, warmer, and more relaxed retirement. The prices would only go higher as Northerners sold their old homes and had large sums of cash to buy Florida houses that were still cheap relative to housing up North. Plenty of price increase was in store for these properties, they all agreed.

Rob provided a couple of real estate contracts so they could make offers. The first property was listed for $650,000, and the second for $525,000. Properties were selling so quickly that Rob suggested they should offer only a few thousand dollars below the listing prices. Alice told Eric she didn't want to risk losing out on getting the properties, but she was preaching to the choir. They filled out the first offer in the amount of $640,000, listing themselves as the buyers. The offer for the second property listed the IRA as the purchaser at the price of $520,000.

> ### How to Buy Property in a Self-Directed IRA
>
> The IRA, by law, requires a bank or trust company to serve as "custodian." This company will serve as an intermediary and hold title of the IRA's assets for your benefit.
>
> The custodian Eric and Alice chose was Pensco Trust Company. To make an offer for the IRA to purchase property, they had to list the buyer as *Pensco Trust Company f/b/o (for benefit of) Eric Fischer IRA.* Then they had to send the contract to the custodian for a custodian's signature on behalf of the buyer, Eric's IRA.

For the first property, they planned on making a five-percent down payment, and obtaining a mortgage loan for the rest. For the other property (which was to be acquired by the IRA), the custodian company advised them that the only way they could legally obtain mortgage financing was to use a "non-recourse" mortgage loan. This meant that they could not personally guarantee the mortgage loan, and the lender typically would usually require a much larger down payment of at least 30 percent. They didn't mind making a larger down payment because it was coming out of IRA money already dedicated to investments. Rob faxed the offers to the seller's real estate agent while Eric and Alice already began planning their vacation schedule. Two days and one counteroffer later, they had two accepted purchase agreements.

Non-Recourse Mortgage Basics

The mortgage loans most of us are accustomed to are "recourse" loans. The property is collateral for the loan, but in the event of a default, the lender can foreclose on the property and exercise the additional recourse of suing the borrower to recover all of what was owed.

In a non-recourse loan, there is no additional recourse beyond foreclosure. This makes the underwriting simpler—there is no need to evaluate a borrower's job or credit because the lender can't go after the borrower anyway. So a non-recourse lender will look more closely at the loan's subject property to ensure that the appraised value is accurate and conservative.

Additionally, a non-recourse loan will typically have a much lower loan-to-value ratio than regular recourse loans. This lowers the risk of the loan

> going into default and gives lenders a better chance of getting all of their money back if they do end up having to foreclose on the property.
>
> Interest rates for a non-recourse loan are fairly competitive, but still are about 0.5 percent to 1.0 percent higher than the rate for a similar recourse loan.

The time was early 2006, and the mortgage financing for the first property was a breeze because of the couple's high credit scores. The non-recourse financing for the second property was just as easy because of the large down payment. They were able to close on both properties in about 30 days and immediately hired the property manager who worked in Rob's office to rent the properties out to other vacationers. Without providing specifics, the property manager projected that the rental income on these properties would bring them just about to the break-even point—not much more, not much less. Eric and Alice were satisfied with this because their real goal was to cash in on the property appreciation. When it came time to close on the purchase of each property, the closing documents were mailed to Eric and Alice in New Jersey to sign and then to forward the documents for the IRA-purchased property to San Francisco for Pensco Trust Company to sign on behalf of Eric's IRA.

Upon closing, here's how the balance sheet for each property looked:

Balance Sheet February 2006					
Assets	**USD**	**MPC**	**Liabilities**	**USD**	**MPC**
Property #1	642,000	642.00	Mortgage loan #1	609,900	609.90
Property #2 (in IRA)	520,000	520.00	Mortgage loan #2	338,000	338.00
Savings account	10,000	10.00			
Cash in IRA	15,000	15.00			
Total Assets	1,187,000	1187.00	Total Liabilities	947,900	947.90
Net Worth	239,100	239.10	*(MPC conversion rate: 1,000)*		

The purpose of their investment in these two properties was to wait for property values to rise. Eric and Alice could then profit by selling the properties, or even by completing a cash-out refinance to borrow against the new equity once it was available. This strategy was simple, and had been successful for many other people before Eric and Alice.

What happened next was devastating. The real estate bubble popped. As it turned out, they weren't investing at all; they were speculating. Their entire profit strategy depended on the homes rising in value. So many people seemed so sure that homes in general would always rise in value every year that Eric and Alice felt confident that their attempt at profiting from real estate was low risk.

When the real estate bubble popped, Florida was among the worst-hit real estate markets. So many other people had played the game of anticipating appreciation that prices had already run up much higher than the homes' actual values. Just like all the others who had purchased Florida real estate during that time, Eric and Alice didn't want to actually pay those prices for those properties—they just wanted to borrow money to own the property for a period of time, and then sell it to someone else for an even higher price. This is known as the "greater fool" method of investing. It is based entirely on the hope that a greater fool than yourself will come along and buy your asset for an even higher price than you paid.

The greater fool theory is what made both the technology stock dot-com bubble and the housing bubble possible. It is the underlying principle of the stock market as we know it today. When the theory is working, it's intoxicating. Making money never seems easier than when you simply buy things and sell them for more. Who cares how the prices and values are calculated? There's very little doubt or regret when you're selling things to the greater fool for heaps more than you paid. However, eventually the *greater* fool is nowhere to be found, and the fool left holding the asset for which he overpaid...is you.

This happened to Eric and Alice. Their investment position was weak. It depended entirely on the presence of greater fools who would remain willing to pay higher and higher prices for no good reason.

In Eric and Alice's case, the cash flow of these properties did not let them break even. They were losing money every month because of their higher mortgage payments. Figuring it was about time to cash out their investment, they hired Rob to list the properties for sale. He started the list prices out much higher than Eric and Alice had paid. After six months, they had not received a single offer on either property, so they paid a licensed appraiser to give them an official opinion of what the properties were worth so that they would know what to expect. When they received the appraisals, they were shocked.

The first property, for which they had paid $642,000, was now worth only $380,000 according to comparable sales. The second property, for which they paid $520,000, was now down to $300,000. Because both mortgage loans had interest-only payments, they had not paid down either of the principal balances.

Let's take a look at how this adds up...

Balance Sheet March 2008					
Assets	**USD**	**MPC**	**Liabilities**	**USD**	**MPC**
Property #1	380,000	304.00	Mortgage loan #1	609,900	487.92
Property #2 (in IRA)	300,000	240.00	Mortgage loan #2	338,000	270.40
Savings account	10,000	8.00			
Cash in IRA	15,000	12.00			
Total Assets	705,000	564.00	Total Liabilities	947,900	758.43
Net Worth	-242,900	-194.32			
Previous Net Worth	239,100	239.10			
Net Worth Change	-482,000	-433.42	*(MPC conversion rate: 1,250)*		
Net Worth Change %	-201%	-181%			

Eric and Alice had negative equity. Even if they had a buyer ready to pay the exact prices on the appraisals, they would still have to come up with $250,000 more in cash just to sell their properties! They simply could not afford to do that. They also could not afford to keep making the mortgage payments. Ultimately, they walked away, their mortgage loans went into default, and the properties went through foreclosure. Eric and Alice lost the $39,000 they had paid for the down payment and closing costs for property number 1, and their credit was ruined for defaulting on the mortgage loan. Eric's IRA had started with $200,000. Between the down payment and closing costs for Property number 2, Eric lost about $185,000--more than 90 percent of his IRA.

Balance Sheet December 2008					
Assets	**USD**	**MPC**	**Liabilities**	**USD**	**MPC**
Savings account	10,000	8.00			
Cash in IRA	15,000	12.00			
Total Assets	25,000	20.00	Total Liabilities	0	0.00
Net Worth	25,000	20.00			
Starting Net Worth	239,100	239.10			
Net Worth Change	-214,100	219.10	*(MPC conversion rate: 1,250)*		
Net Worth Change %	-89.54%	-91.64%			

Walking away from the mortgage loans and accepting foreclosure actually improved their net worth by forcing the mortgage lender to face its share of the losses from the bad loan. Even so, Eric & Alice had lost the majority of what they had started with. If the IRA's remaining cash had been in the stock market, it would have made their results worse as they would have been subject to the stock market collapse in late 2008.

The Lesson

Investing for appreciation is often not investing at all. Rather it is a form of speculation that has repeatedly taken hold of working-class people, sending them into an intoxicating frenzy. The something-for-nothing mentality is like gambling—it draws people in with promises of push-button wealth, then chews them up and spits them out, teaching them an expensive lesson that is usually forgotten a few years later. When asset prices are fueled mostly by hope, there is always a stopping point or peak—after which prices tumble back down to (and sometimes below) the assets' real values.

Buy Low, Get High

"He that lives upon hope will die fasting."
- Albert Einstein

Something terrible has happened in the minds of investors, but something terrific can happen now to fix it. Investors have fallen into thinking that investing is a matter of buying things low and selling them high. In truth, they are buying low and *getting* high on hope. I aim to convince you that an investment strategy focused on *income* instead of gains is possible, less risky, more rewarding, and on top of that, it's the way real investors have been doing things since the beginning of time.

While buying something for one price and selling it for a higher price is profitable, it carries the risk of the asset going down in value. What's more, with the incessant inflation of 1971 and beyond, an asset can actually go down in value while going up in price. Investors thus celebrate gains that are truly losses, as discussed earlier. This chronic inflationary force is partly to blame for the common belief that conventional investments are on a constant trek upward in value. Measuring properly (step 1 of the 5 steps to freedom) shows you that conventional investments *are* on a constant path upward in dollar-based *price*, but that's only because the dollar is constantly losing its purchasing power. Longer investment periods endure larger amounts of inflation. This is why "holding on for the long term" is the axiom of the conventional investment mindset—it appears to work when you look at the prices. **But it is only by decades of not pay-ing attention to inflation that you find the appearance of wealth growth through conventional methods.**

Another reason for the focus on gains is the gambling mindset. The more risk a person takes, the more luck be-comes a requisite for success. One person takes enormous risk and achieves enormous gains. Then his story plays on the minds of many others who desire similar enormous gains for themselves. The original reason a person would start a business was to enjoy its income. The original reason why an investor would buy stock in another person's busi-ness was to enjoy a share of that income. Even on stock ex-changes, the original focus was to give investors access to *dividends*.

But what would happen if an investor who bought stock in order to receive dividends watched the stock price double in a short period of time? He would sell the stock, of course! He could then buy twice as many other dividend-paying stocks. Another (more destructive) thing happens though— the investor believes the process can be repeated. Instead of crediting his huge gain to luck, he credits it to his own abili-ties, or to the marketplace itself. He spreads the word to his friends and family, some of whom join in on the game. When more people join in on the game, and stocks go up even more, it seems to verify that this movement is long term, predictable market performance.

As investors paid less and less attention to dividends, the owners and officers of some publicly-traded companies discovered something profound: if they paid smaller divi-dends to investors, more money would be left over for internal reinvestment in company expansion and growth. This resulted in increased stock price appreciation. Sane, logical, and successful investors focused on buying *dividend income streams* had become transformed into greedy, something-for-nothing-seeking speculators focused on *price.* Owners and officers of publicly-traded companies didn't mind. This shift from investing for income toward speculating for gains meant that those owners and officers could let the stock prices of their own companies shoot up, giving *them* the opportunity to sell for larger, more rapid profits as well.

Soon, investors stopped caring about how healthy and sound a company was, and started caring about how rapidly it could grow and how rapidly the stock price would increase. Once investors refocused attention from dividends to price trends, there was no longer a good way to calculate a good price for a stock. Previously, an investor seeking a 10 percent ROI would look for stocks selling at or below 10 times their annual dividend. If XYZ Corporation paid dividends of $10 per share, the 10-percent investor would buy XYZ Corporation for any price under $100 per share. In this kind of understandable, logical marketplace, stable, healthy and sound companies were available for investors to buy into.

Once investors turned into wide-eyed speculators, though, they replaced the price-to-dividend ratios of stocks with price-to-earnings ratios. The former tells an investor what income he *is going* to receive from owning a stock, while the latter focuses only on what income the investor *could have* received from owning a stock. A company could have a hugely profitable year and share only peanuts with its shareholders. The speculator doesn't care about this, because he hopes that the company will invest the dividends it didn't pay into huge growth initiatives so that he can sell his stock for much more than he paid for it.

What is a good price-to-earnings (P/E) ratio? Who knows? Back when dividends mattered more, each investor chose his own price-to-dividends ratio based on his desired ROI. That ratio equated to the investor's profit. P/E, on the other hand doesn't equate to anything. Speculative pundits say all kinds of things about this company or that company trading at a high or a low P/E that will eventually be corrected. The problem is that bigger isn't always better, as AIG and WaMu have recently taught us. For P/E to mean anything, you have to set your tunnel vision on *growth* and assume that bigger is always better. With speculators looking at a number that doesn't even matter, it's no wonder that the stock market exhibits inexplicable and unpredictable volatility.

This maniacal obsession with growth, appreciation, and gain is not unique to the stock market. You'll find it anywhere people are trying to get something for nothing. Something for something just never seems quite as appealing as something for nothing, and real estate is no exception.

The evolution of how the common speculator has come to treat real estate is not much different from the story of the how the stock market became bastardized. Real investors bought real estate to enjoy its income. An investor seeking a 10 percent return could buy real estate for 10 times its annual income. Then a few things happened. First, people who wanted to become owners of beautiful properties in beautiful locations started showing their pride of ownership by paying prices that carried a lower income-based ROI.

For instance, a one-bedroom condo in Kansas might rent for $600 and have a net income of $4,800 per year. The 10 percent investor will be willing to pay $48,000 for this condo. An identical condo might exist in Miami, Florida, rent for $1,200 per month, and have a net income of $10,800 per year. So the buyer of the condo in Miami should pay $108,000, right? Yes, he should, but he instead pays much more and becomes a 5-percent investor or maybe even a 2-percent investor. Why is he willing to be a 2-percent investor? Because he's not even calculating his income or ROI—he's instead being a "blue water investor." He stares at the blue water out of his window and is so mesmerized he does not even pull out a calculator to see what he's doing financially.

Pride of ownership doesn't wreak havoc on real estate markets by itself. It just means that beautiful properties in beautiful locations carry a premium. Another way to put it is that they are less profitable for the income investor. This is just the setup.

Fast forward to 2001. The United States was in a recession. The Fed took it upon itself to start manipulating interest rates downward. I say manipulate because a free market would have allowed lenders and borrowers to determine the price (interest rate) of borrowed money. In the United States, however, this function of a free market does not exist in lending. Instead, the Fed sets interest rates, and they will always be somewhat higher or lower than where the market would have set them. The Fed really didn't want us to endure a recession, so it kept lowering interest rates over and over to "stimulate the economy" until interest rates were brought to unusually low levels.

Once interest rates are at unusually low levels, *investors* face a dilemma. Previously, an investor was able to get a considerable return virtually "risk-free" by investing his money into a CD or other similar instrument. Lowering interest rates lowered the risk-free returns of CDs to levels unsatisfactory to investors. How did investors respond? By taking on risk. And it just so happened that at that very moment, real estate seemed to be "a bull"[19] worthy of risk.

By the time investors decided to take on more risk, lower interest rates had already had a curious effect on residential real estate prices. Most homebuyers in modern times don't pay cash, so the home they can afford is a function of the monthly mortgage payment they can afford. When the interest portion of that payment shrinks, the principal portion will take its place. So if Sally Homebuyer can afford a $1,000 mortgage payment and lowered interest rates cut out $200 of her monthly mortgage expense, she can then afford to pay more for a home with the same $1000 mortgage payment.

This artificial, Fed-concocted housing price increase then turned real estate agents into the same repetitive zombies that stock brokers had been for decades—touting the conventional wisdom that "the market always goes up over

---

[19] A good general rule I follow is to run in the other direction if I ever hear a person use the words "bull" or "bear" to refer to anything other than an actual wild animal. It's a sign that the person has such a weak understanding of investing that they only focus on price trends. This *especially* applies to "expert" commentary.

time." Now, as covered earlier, *all* markets appear to go up over time when you measure prices in declining dollars. But the interest-rate-cut shenanigans gave the real estate industry an added boost.

"Wow, I can just buy real estate now and sell it later for a profit since it's always going up," thought the first guy who accidentally received enormous gains. Then he told his friends and family, some of whom jumped into the game. Of course, the influx of real estate buyers looking to cash in on gains pushed prices further upward. When the question, "Do we have a bubble here?" was first uttered, the mortgage industry insisted, "NO!" as it proceeded to roll out a series of unbelievably stupid loan programs. No income verification, no job verification, no asset or reserves verification; some didn't even require a social security number.

Yet all these risk parameters were ignored at unbelievable leverage ratios: 95 percent LTV, 100 percent LTV, even 120 percent LTV! I know this because I used to own a mortgage company and each month, "account executives" from various mortgage lenders came to my office to promote increasingly brainless loan programs that could end in no way other than non-payment.

Many regular people found themselves sucked into this game. Well that game is over, and I now often hear regular people react to real estate investing by saying, "Well, gosh, the real estate market is so bad right now; it's certainly time to wait it out." What's really so bad right now is the bubble game or the outlook for those using the greater fool theory. Real estate *investing* has been available to moguls and regular people alike throughout the past few decades, regardless of price swings.

People have been buying income-producing property for favorable prices for the entire period. The real fluctuations are in how much work is required in order to actually buy an income-producing property for a favorable price. At the height of the bubble, real estate buying operating on the greater fool theory bid prices up so high that it made it difficult for a real investor to buy properties at advantageous prices (with a desirable price-to-income ratio).

The bursting of the housing bubble has made buying property at favorable prices easier again. In fact, as millions of families return to renting after being stung by Fannie Mae's *dream of home ownership for everyone*, rental properties in many areas are experiencing an unexpected increase in rental rates. This only magnifies the ROI for the real investor who owns the rental properties, as the next case study illustrates.

CASE STUDY:
Income vs. Gains

Carol had never met anyone who had built substantial wealth by putting his or her savings into the stock market. On the other hand, she had met many people who had built wealth by investing in real estate. Figuring this wasn't mere coincidence, Carol decided to start buying income-producing homes.

She lived in San Francisco and started looking around town. Her friend Kenny, along with most other real estate investors, was only speculating for gains. These speculators had run prices up so high that, by her estimate, she could expect rental income to produce a return of only five percent per year or less. These investors didn't care about the unfavorable price-to-income ratio because they paid attention only to asset appreciation. Carol didn't want her investment strategy to depend on prices that she couldn't control, so she shifted her sights to the area where she grew up and where home prices weren't bloated—Missouri.

Back in Missouri, home prices were not unexplainably shooting up. There was just a relatively stable marketplace. So she setup her Solo 401(k) and took a trip to St. Louis, where a referred real estate agent awaited her. After looking at about eight properties, Carol took a closer look at the one with the best numbers. It was a single-family home listed for sale for $75,000 with a renter paying $800 per month already in place. The following table breaks down her financial calculations.

$9,600	Gross annual income
($679)	Insurance premiums
($742)	Property taxes
($576)	Annual maintenance & repairs
($960)	Management fee (10% of rents)
$6,643	Net Operating Income

$75,000	Purchase price
$6,643	Net operating income
8.85%	Return on investment

This was a decent ROI, especially considering the miniscule risk. There wasn't a lot of building going on in the area to change the supply. The demand for housing would stay about the same as long as the population and job market didn't drastically change. So Carol decided to add a bit of leverage in the form of a non-recourse mortgage loan. Let's see how it improved her cash-on-cash ROI:[20]

$75,000	Purchase price
$48,750	Loan amount
$26,250	Down payment
65%	Loan-to-value
5.75%	Interest rate
$2,803	Interest-only payments (annual total)

---

[20] Creating leverage by borrowing money will magnify profits if your total ROI is higher than the interest rate of the loan. On the flip side, if the investment creates losses, leverage will magnify them as well.

$75,000	Purchase price
$6,643	Net operating income
$2,803	Debt payments
$3,839	Profit (after debt service)
$28,770	Cash invested (down pmt + closing costs)
13.34%	Cash-on-cash ROI

These projections looked good to her, so she moved forward and bought the property. Because negotiating brought her purchase price a couple thousand lower than the asking price, her projected ROI actually increased to just below 14 percent. Carol didn't break the bank with enormous profits, but her solid 14 percent ROI was nothing to shake a stick at. While house prices in some areas may swing violently, rents are normally much more stable. Because Carol's profits were derived from rents, they were stable, because people need places to live. Carol steadily acquired more properties with similar ROIs. After her first acquisition, she was comfortable enough with her real estate agent, pre-purchase property inspector, appraiser, and property manager to acquire most of her future properties without making a trip to see them in person.

As other examples in this book show, there are many ways to build wealth more rapidly than 14 percent per year. But in Carol's case, a minimal amount of skill and effort was required to create that ROI. The real estate agent did all the searching. The appraiser verified the property's value and confirmed that its rental income was in line with the rest of the local rental market. The property inspector helped her understand the condition of the property and alerted her to any major problems the appraiser didn't look for. The property manager did all the work of screening renters, signing leases, ordering repairs, and dealing with the general affairs of the property.

Carol's Solo 401(k) purchased it. Carol's role was simply to select the members of her team of real estate professionals, to calculate net operating income (NOI) and cash-on-cash return, and to make the final decisions. The risk lay in the possibility that one of the team members might slip up or overlook something important. Carol's risk would have been greater if she had just opened up the yellow pages to build her real estate team, but she networked through other successful local investors and asked for referrals to build her team. She asked for referrals from *successful investors* whose experience and track record went well beyond house flipping. A referral from anyone else would have been no more valuable than a listing in the phone book.

Another important factor is that Carol did not limit herself to buying properties only where she lived. Had she done that, she would have been stuck buying $800,000 homes and creating an ROI of about 3 percent—less than breaking even after inflation. She was not misdirected by the news media, which talk about the performance of markets as a whole. It is far too easy to assume that news reporting has meaning with regard to investing in any specific market. The "real estate market" as a whole has no direct connection to the profits created by investing in *specific* properties. Her friend Kenny invested in "the real estate market" in San Francisco and created returns of 2 to 5 percent. Carol, on the other hand, created returns of 12 to 15 percent.[21] Were they both in the same "real estate market"?

True investors don't buy markets; they buy assets. One person may decide against real estate investing because prices in the whole real estate market are on the decline, while another person may buy mutual funds and index funds in belief that the whole stock market produces reliable profit. Both would be making the same mistake—buying markets instead of individual assets. True diversification is a matter of buying more than one asset—*not* buying an investment package like a mutual fund or index fund.

Anyone can do what Carol did. If you are willing to work for money, you should be just as willing to put your money to work for you. As a starting point, put one or more income-producing properties in your investment portfolio. If a 14-percent return satisfies your wealth-building goals, you don't have to go beyond Carol's simple strategy. To grow your wealth more rapidly, however, you'll need to purchase additional assets, such as opportunistic investments in high-margin development projects as in our next case study.

---

[21] Balance sheets were not provided with this case study because the focus was on income-producing properties. As inflation grows in the coming years, there is a good chance rents will increase accordingly. As a result, Carols ROI wouldn't be harshly affected by inflation, and she would confirm this by periodically preparing a balance sheet and cash flow statement.

CASE STUDY:
Peruvian Profits

There are many different ways to react to our crumbling American economy. You can be angry. You can do nothing. You can complain. You can deny our nation's financial problems. Or, you can start searching for a healthier economy to invest in.[22] That's exactly what airline pilot Bob Stoll did, and he earned a 45 percent return in only 15 months.

Stoll believed in making his money available for the right investment opportunity. After doing some research, he decided to open a self-directed IRA and rollover his $250,000 in retirement funds. After being introduced to a Peruvian real estate developer, Bob was given an opportunity to contribute to funding housing development in Lima, Peru and reap remarkable returns.

The Development

The project was a 64-unit building consisting of one-, two-, and three-bedroom condos ranging in size from 600 to 900 square feet, and selling for an average of $120,000. Investors could invest in various phases of the development, rather than purchasing individual condo units.

---

[22] There's no shame in investing in other countries. Don't let anyone convince you that the wealth of our country is anything other than what its people hold.

"I learned that there are thousands of people in Lima who are pre-approved to buy homes, but there's not enough supply," said Bob. Local banks had lengthy lists of pre-approved clients waiting for homes. The developer can learn precisely where the demand is. "We go to the bank and say 'What do you need us to fulfill?' and they tell us that they have a number of people at this price point who are looking for a home in a particular area. So they tell us, 'If you can build something in that area we can sell it,'" explained Felipe Martinez, the real estate developer whom Bob invests with.

Stoll invested $200,000 using his self-directed IRA. The LLC raised $1.5 million for the equity portion of the project, and each investor received his capital back, along with a sizeable profit, in less than a year and a half. At the heart of Stoll's decision to invest with Felipe was the stable growth of Peru's economy.

Why Peru?

It's a good question, because many of us think of Latin America in recent decades as nothing more than an unstable, politically corrupt, poverty-stricken, limited-growth group of countries. Today, only a person who has never visited Lima or inquired into facts could think that. Those who have explored and researched the situation have become part of the changes that are revealing a new, brighter side of Latin America. The growth patterns in Peru are similar to the developmental progress in Chile several years ago.

So, why Peru? The answer is simple. Its economy is experiencing healthy growth that has created a high profit margin for real estate development. Peru experienced an 8.9 percent Gross Domestic Product (GDP) increase in 2008; that's among the highest increases in the world. In the last 10 years, Peru has enjoyed the greatest economic growth in its history. Three factors have significantly contributed to this transformation: a stable government, sound foreign investment, and a rapidly expanding middle class.

This expanding middle class is creating great demand for new housing, and that, in turn, is being encouraged by Peruvian banks that are willing to offer mortgage loans with 20 to 30 percent down.

Still more evidence of Peru's encouraging economic growth potential comes from its increasing Net International Reserves, which recently grew in value by 16.6 percent to $31 billion USD. Just last year, Fitch Ratings and Standard & Poor's upgraded Peru to investment grade, and in 2007 Peru and the United States completed a Free Trade Agreement (FTA). Similar agreements with Canada, Thailand, China, and Singapore are already in place. Additional negotiations for new agreements are in process with the European Union and pending with Mexico.

Another economic development on the horizon is Peru LNG (Liquefied Natural Gas), a $3.8 billion project. It is expected to support economic growth in some of Peru's poorest regions and will be the largest foreign direct investment in the country's history.

After operations begin in 2010, the project is expected to extract and process Peruvian natural gas resources in excess of local demand. It is also expected to increase the country's total exports by an estimated 1.5 percent, and make Peru a net hydrocarbon exporter.

You may be wondering how the global credit crisis, which is a primary concern of investors throughout the world, will affect Peru. The country is expected to experience slowing growth in exports and in select commodity markets, but sustained internal growth leaves Peru positioned fairly well in these difficult economic times.

In the summer of 2007, Stoll invested into Felipe's project to develop condominiums in a moderate-income neighborhood. Let's take a look at how he earned his nearly 50 percent return in 15 months.

Balance Sheet August 2007					
Assets	USD	MPC	Liabilities	USD	MPC
Cash in IRA	50,000	50.00			
Peru investment	200,000	200.00			
Total Assets	250,000	250.00	Total Liabilities	0	0.00
Net Worth	250,000	250.00	(MPC conversion rate: 1,000)		

Peru's housing needs are tremendous. Felipe's focus was on building housing for the middle class. "People who are making $40,000 to $70,000 make up the middle class," said Felipe.

There are 43 districts in Lima; Felipe works in seven of them. "In Peru, efficiency is important. They don't need a lot of room and they don't need a lot of amenities. They just need a comfortable, efficient place to live," said Felipe. So that's exactly what he develops.

Stoll was introduced to Felipe and the opportunity to invest in the Peruvian condo project through networking with other investors. He reviewed the economic state of Peru and invested his money. Once construction began, the turnaround for profit was fast. Stoll received his capital back plus a $90,000 profit in 15 months. The condos were completely sold out before the project was finished.

Balance Sheet November 2008					
Assets	**USD**	**MPC**	**Liabilities**	**USD**	**MPC**
Cash in IRA	340,000	309.09			
Total Assets	340,000	309.09	Total Liabilities	0	0.00
Net Worth	340,000	309.09			
Previous Net Worth	250,000	250.00			
Net Worth Change	+90,000	+59.09	*(MPC conversion rate: 1,100)*		
Net Worth Change %	+36.00%	+23.64%			

One of the big concerns when you're investing money in a project that's being built in a foreign country is how cooperative the government will be with the development and its investors. "Peru is listed among the highest countries on the protecting investors index in Latin America. They want investors. They'll do anything they can to help foreign investors," said Felipe. He adds that there is no difference between United States and Peruvian investors—both have the same rights.

However, investing in real estate, whether in the United States or another country, requires doing due diligence. Stoll looked into Felipe's track record and verified his claims in order to be certain he had been consistently delivering what he predicted. He also talked with Felipe's other investors to get their feedback about the project. You can learn a lot from investors who have traveled to the country to view the development sites.

Then you weigh your risk. The worst-case scenario is that the building doesn't sell as expected. If it sells significantly less than anticipated, it is possible for investors to lose their money. You need to make sure you are investing your money with a developer who understands the country and has the right connections with the banks and government to ensure that the project will sell as anticipated.

The most notable feature of Stoll's story is how the source of profit in this project is different from most recent construction projects in the US—at least for the individual investor. In the United States, countless investors have bought condo units themselves, distorting the purchase price because the buyers didn't want to be the ultimate owners. Profits were to come from reselling the condo for a higher price.

In Felipe's project, on the other hand, the condo buyers were the people who wanted to own and occupy them. Additionally, the profit from Felipe's project was based on a construction profit margin—selling all the condos brought in much more money than the cost to construct them. Felipe raised the funds needed to construct the building and shared the profits with his investors. His strategy did not depend on tourists or vacationers. Nor did it depend on prices going up or on unrealistic mortgage loan programs. Buyers put 20 percent or more down and proved their incomes.

Of further interest, the Peruvian government has a fiscal surplus and the nation maintains a trade surplus. For most every negative economic indicator in the United States, Peru has an inversely positive one. While the Fed has been printing trillions of dollars, the Peruvian central bank has raised reserve requirements several times, which contracts their money supply.

Thinking outside of the box may sometimes involve thinking outside of the country.

CASE STUDY:
Grande Dunes

Jake is a likeable, good-looking guy, He typically arrives in a Porsche with a nice tan and pearly white teeth. He has a good sense of humor and a charming smile, but what steers his life is his need to impress others. He feels a strong need to be as rich as possible as quickly as possible, so that all the friends he makes can come over to congratulate him and enjoy the hot tub in his mansion.

On cue, when the real estate boom arrived, Jake dove in. I know this story well because Jake worked for me in the mortgage business. He did well because he was good at creating relationships. People will do business with people they like, and Jake was a likeable guy. Within a few months, he was making over $20,000 per month.

I had read about real estate investing and started buying duplexes for $80,000 and collecting $1,000 per month in rent. They produced strong cash flows at 20 percent down. I encouraged Jake to look into real estate investing, but he looked in a far different place. He had been originating mortgage loans on huge beachfront homes for a local developer. That developer seemed to be making more money than anyone he knew, so Jake decided to imitate him.

As I continued searching for small, affordable duplexes, Jake set his eyes on the ultimate place to build homes: Grande Dunes in Myrtle Beach, South Carolina. This was the neighborhood where all the doctors lived. To enter the neighborhood, you had to drive over the intercoastal waterway on a private $7 million bridge. After passing two security points, one manned and one electronic, you could finally raise your nose triumphantly up into the air—you had arrived.

At least, that's how it started. By the time events ran their course, the neighborhood had become home to unemployed waitresses and anyone else willing to take a "liar's loan",[23] while beautiful and stunning houses sat unoccupied amid dozens of construction projects. But let's not get ahead of ourselves.

Jake figured that if real estate prices were going up, then dealing in the most expensive properties would bring the most profit. He felt he could build a home for $200,000 and sell it for $250,000, or he could build a home for $2 million and sell it for $2.5 million. With a mental image of his hot tub overflowing with beautiful women who appreciated a rich guy like the one Jake would become, he chose the latter. It just seemed so much easier to make $500,000 by doing one deal instead of ten.

So Jake put a deposit down on a lot in the Grande Dunes neighborhood. He partnered with a builder who would build the home and share in the profits. This was a formula that could be duplicated, and Jake couldn't resist building several of these $2 million homes.

---

[23] Also known as stated income and stated asset, these loans invited the borrower to simply state their income and assets without providing supporting documentation. No matter how innocent their original intentions, these loan programs ultimately became a tool for real estate speculators to buy homes they couldn't afford.

I warned Jake almost daily of the insanity he was wallowing in. But Jake didn't want to hear it, so he left and started his own mortgage company. Even though we didn't keep in touch, keeping tabs on him was easy enough in a small resort town. Soon enough, Jake got his mansion and it was overflowing with beautiful women… temporarily.

He had two homes under construction, but he still couldn't get enough. He started partnering with other people to acquire the lots by having them put up the money and the credit. Some of our mutual friends came to me for advice. Should they invest with Jake? My answer was always "no." I had read John Rubino's book, *How To Profit From The Coming Real Estate Bust*. It made sense to me, and one thing it *didn't* recommend was to put all of your money and credit into building multi-million dollar homes.

Some of these friends listened, and some didn't. If Jake had just saved half the money he made from the bubble, he could have kept on living a normal life afterward. But he was consumed by the allure of something-for-nothing real estate riches. It seemed like everything was out there for the taking, and he wanted to take as much as possible for himself.

When the boom turned into a bust, he was left holding several $2 million homes. The mortgage payment on the home he lived in was over $5,000 per month. He had to pay another $20,000-plus in mortgage payments per month once he was stuck with the other homes. Waiting it out for a few months cost him nearly all the cash he had.

He was sitting in a magnificent luxury home with his Porsches and Mercedes parked in front, yet he couldn't afford to buy groceries or put gas in his cars. Throughout the country, thousands of other high rollers were in similar situations.

Jake had gotten a taste of the lifestyle of the rich and famous, and he didn't want to go back to being just an ordinary guy. When I first recruited him four years earlier, he was a personal fitness trainer living in a small apartment and driving a $3,000 car. Now he found himself needing $10,000 per week just to stay above water.

He needed to wipe the slate clean. Unfortunately, he had "special circumstances," so for him, wiping the slate clean was... well, special. The circle he ran in was full of guys who loved to gamble on sports. Jake fit right in, as he also loved to gamble on sports, and this was a problem. By the time he needed to wipe the slate clean, he owed hundreds of thousands of dollars to bookies. While the banks that gave him mortgage loans would accept their losses on Jake, the bookies would not. His health and maybe even his life depended on paying these bookies.

I was told Jake reacted to the situation by convincing a farmer to give him $300,000 for a real estate investment, and then disappearing. I haven't seen him, and I don't know anybody else who has. He's probably either living under a different name, hiding, or dead. This is a bubble story of fantastic proportions, but at the root it's the same as every other bubble story.

Each investment Jake made was 1 percent investment and 99 percent speculation. His positions were weak. For each of his deals to turn out profitable, some ridiculous assumptions had to come true. Banks had to keep making bad loans. Buyers had to keep buying homes they couldn't afford. It simply isn't possible for those two phenomena to continue indefinitely.

Some people say greed is behind bubbles, but it's not that simple. A *smart* greedy person would have ended up rich. He would have entered into strong positions instead of weak ones. He would have acknowledged his assumptions and projected their risks or estimated the length of time that the assumptions would work. Greed is not to blame for bubbles—intoxication[24] is. Jake and all the other speculators who patted themselves on the back while unknowingly skipping down the path to foreclosure and bankruptcy were simply drunk out of their minds.

---

[24] In the real estate bubble, the drug of choice was a cocktail made of one part Fed-created money supply; one part easy mortgage loans provided by Fannie Mae and Freddie Mac; one part outright lies from risk ratings agencies which convinced investors to buy mortgage-backed securities by misrepresenting their risk; and one part the press inviting everyone to the party and feeding them the punch.

CASE STUDY:
ROBS: Really Outrageously Bad Strategy

Chris worked in a cubicle. He'd been working various jobs for 25 years and always dreamed of starting his own business, but he never knew where to start. Then, one day, he was reading a magazine that promoted buying franchises. According to one article, starting a business was a risky affair. On the other hand, a franchise was a business system that you could purchase instead of creating your own. A franchisor develops a system and sells the rights to an entrepreneur, the franchisee, to run a business that uses the branding, software, marketing, vendor relationships, and the entire business system. The franchisee pays an up-front fee and a percentage of ongoing revenues to the franchisor.

This sounded great to Chris, even though he had never started or run a business before. His only problem was finding the startup funds. Like many people, Chris didn't have much savings beyond his emergency fund and a $250,000 IRA. Nevertheless, he continued browsing through franchise Web sites and eventually settled on a print shop franchise.

When contacting the franchisor to get more information, Chris told them about his predicament with funds. No need to worry, he was told—there are companies that specialized in setting up creative structures to fund business startups. There was Guidant Financial's Audeo product, Benetrends' Rainmaker Plan, the ERSOP, and many others. They are all essentially the same product.

The Qualifying Employer Securities (QES) 401(k) Structure

1. A corporation is formed.
2. The new C corporation adopts a 401(k) plan.
3. The entrepreneur is a participant in the 401(k) plan and rolls over funds from his existing retirement accounts into this new plan.
4. Once his 401(k) account is funded, he directs his 401(k) account to purchase stock in the corporation.
5. His retirement funds are ultimately in the hands of the corporation he runs. He then uses these funds to start the business. The entrepreneur draws a salary from the corporation.

If you have a basic understanding of "prohibited transactions" as they pertain to retirement plans (discussed in more detail later in the book), this may jump out at you as a prohibited transaction. The plan participant and most of his or her family members are "disqualified persons," as are any entities (such as an LLC or corporation) in which a disqualified person has significant ownership. A prohibited transaction is one where a plan transacts with a disqualified person.

However, the Internal Revenue Code provides an exemption to prohibited transactions for the acquisition of "qualifying employer securities" or "QES." QES are stock in the employer who has adopted a plan where the stock is purchased for its appraised value and represents ownership in a C corporation. After the money goes from the 401(k) into the C corporation, it becomes the C corporation's money, and the prohibited transaction rules are allegedly no longer applicable.

So, Chris setup a QES 401(k) with one of the providers he was referred to. He paid $5,000 and received a records binder for a C corporation and a 401(k) plan. After the rollover of IRA funds into the 401(k) was completed, he directed the plan to purchase 95 percent of the corporation's stock for $200,000 and ended up running a corporation that had that $200,000 in its checking account.

Then he turned to finalizing matters with the franchisor. Chris had settled on buying the printing franchise. The total cost was around $900,000, but with most of the equipment financed through leasing, he required only the $200,000 to start it up. The franchisor helped select the location and negotiate the leasing of the space. It was in a high traffic area, and Chris couldn't wait to get it up and running. He imagined all of the print jobs that would be running through his shop—business cards, flyers, banners, signs, brochures, etc.

Six months later, it was up and running. Chris had traveled to the franchisor's corporate offices for training. His leased space was built to his specifications. His equipment was delivered. He had signs in place and ads in the yellow pages, and he hired a couple of employees to help him out.

Ultimately, Chris's business failed. Expenses outweighed revenues, and it didn't turn around in time. He didn't know why, because he'd never had any successful business experience to draw from. Chris put far too much faith in the business system. The official disclosure document, the Uniform Franchise Offering Circular (UFOC), seemed like a formality that was less important than his other communications with the franchisor; so he didn't review it carefully.

Many franchisors fail to give their potential franchisees realistic expectations. In fact, the International Franchise Association (IFA) recently sent a letter[25] to all of its franchisor members demanding that they stop quoting an outdated study from 1987 that claimed buying a franchise was less risky and had a higher success rate than non-franchise startups. That might have been true when the study was conducted. But franchising grew in popularity throughout the 1990s and beyond. It provided a great alternative to entrepreneurs who wanted to expand their business. Rather than raising money from investors to open more locations, many entrepreneurs became franchisors and recruited other entrepreneurs to buy franchises and operate in new business locations. Becoming a franchisor costs about $50,000 in legal fees, and the franchisor can then publicly advertise its opportunity. By contrast, expanding business by raising capital from investors in the public equity market costs over $1 million. For these reasons, franchising exploded in popularity.

So many franchise opportunities popped up that it was no longer true that "franchising was less risky and held a higher rate of success" than non-franchise startup businesses. That didn't stop franchisors from continuing to market their franchises as less risky than non-franchise startups.

No one knows how effective the IFA letter to its members was, but today the fallacious idea that buying a franchise offers a higher chance of success than starting a business from scratch is still prevalent. Chris was trapped by

---

[25] Letter from President Matthew Shay to IFA members, dated 5/2/2005.

this fallacy, and it cost him 80 percent of his retirement funds.

I am not saying "don't start a business." On the contrary, if you haven't started a business yet, you should start one. Even if you are a full-time employee at someone else's company, I think you should start a business on the side. Business ownership is the only shortcut to wealth. Unless you're 18 years old and willing to work diligently for an employer for 40 years, you have but two main paths to wealth. One is to invest your assets to achieve extraordinary returns. The other is business ownership. All the better to combine both.

But don't start a business with money that you aren't prepared to lose. Statistically, a new small business doesn't have good odds of success. According to the Department of Commerce, the vast majority of small businesses fail within a few years. So why even try? The logic is simple.

I've been an entrepreneur for eight years. I have friends who are also entrepreneurs, and some of them have had success greater than I've ever dreamed. I've found there is a single unifying characteristic among all successful entrepreneurs: a willingness to fail. Ordinary people see failure as a buzzer at the end of a losing basketball game at the end of a season or a career, and are afraid of failure and avoid it at all costs.

Successful entrepreneurs, on the other hand, recognize failures as stepping-stones on the path to success. They are either *willing to fail* or unwilling to acknowledge their failures. Thomas Edison failed thousands of times in his attempts to make a working light bulb. When asked how he persevered through those thousands of failures, he replied that he hadn't failed at all; rather he had successfully made thousands of light bulbs that didn't light up before making one that did. And Charles Kettering, inventor of the electric automobile starter, said, "An inventor fails 999 times, and if he succeeds once, he's in. He treats his failures simply as practice shots."

If Chris's path to success had been anything like that of most successful entrepreneurs, it would have been peppered with failures. Only one person can declare Chris a Failure with a capital "F," and that's Chris himself. If he's flexible and allows his plans to evolve, he can push through to success. He might have to round up funding more than once. It may take longer than expected to get the business "out of the red" and past the point of profitability. He might have to try something different from what was in the original business plan.[26] He might have to do whatever it takes.

Sometimes what it takes is more money. Had he been true to the philosophy behind diversification, Chris's first business would have been partially funded by Chris and partially funded by his friends, family, and other contacts. If that first business failed, Chris could have afforded to dust himself off and get up to start another business. In fact, his co-investors might have been happy to invest with him again.

Chris could also have included a successful entrepreneur on his team. Most successful and wealthy people are

---

[26] Many of the most famous business successes started out selling one product or service and switched to a completely different product or service in order to become successful. For examples, I recommend reading *Founders at Work* by Jessica Livingston.

driven to give back to others in appreciation for achieving their own success. What I've accomplished in my own entrepreneurial endeavors would not have been possible without the help of my mentors.

In fact, Chris can still dust himself off and start another business. All this talk of perseverance still holds true, but a key lesson in his story is to not pay so much of your own money for your initial failures, lessons, or stepping-stones.

Another important dimension of Chris's story is his legal compliance. Chris used a "QES 401(k)" structure to invest his retirement funds in his business rather than distributing the funds to himself, paying the taxes, and then investing the remaining funds into the business launch. Understanding the compliance issues related to Self-Directed IRA & 401(k) strategies can be difficult. This is partly because the IRS has authority over certain issues and the Department of Labor (DOL) has jurisdiction over others. Companies offering to set up a QES 401(k) have been around since the 1990s. Thousands of these structures have been set up. But in October of 2008, the IRS started publicly cracking down on certain compliance issues. The biggest question is "Is the QES 401(k) a legitimate and compliant strategy?" The IRS can't fully answer that question, because prohibited transactions for retirement accounts are the domain of the DOL and have been since 1978.

I meet with DOL agents each year in Washington, D.C. to further my understanding of the ever-changing rules about prohibited transactions. In December of 2008, my DOL meeting brought an unexpected surprise: the DOL believes that the QES 401(k) structure is a prohibited transaction.[27]

This came as a surprise because I know several attorneys who are very comfortable and confident in their promotion of the QES 401(k) strategy. One of them has set up thousands of these. By the time you have read this book, the DOL will probably have issued official guidance to put the issue to rest. Meanwhile, later in the book, I'll list additional resources for further researching the topic.

Chris did do something commendable. He took the leap of entrepreneurship. That's the hardest part. He made mistakes by ignoring diversification, thinking that buying a franchise is low risk, and, ultimately, using an investment structure that was prohibited by law.

If I could take Chris back in a time machine to his initial decisions, I would suggest he follow a different path. Let's assume Chris found a mentor, received his mentor's approval for a business plan that didn't require hiring full-time employees, and still needed $200,000 to start the business. I would propose that Chris's new business adopt a Solo 401(k) plan, and he transfer his existing retirement funds into the new plan. From this point, Chris could take a participant loan of up to $50,000 and use the funds for any purpose. He could then contribute the funds to the new business and find three other people to also invest $50,000 into the business.

---

[27] At the time of writing the DOL has not yet released an official opinion on the compliance of the QES 401(k) specifically, but previous opinions, when applied to the QES 401(k), classify it as a prohibited transaction punishable by a 100 percent tax.

For Chris to raise money from others, he has to be convincing in his pitch. The act of raising money can be fruitful beyond just raising money, especially if it forces him to be more thorough in his business planning. This may oblige him to be more specific in his goals and how he aims to reach them. If Chris can't convince three other people to invest $50,000 in a new business plan, then maybe he shouldn't invest either.

But if Chris does what it takes to satisfy three other investors, then he's launched his business with better diversification and a better business plan, without forcing it into a questionable or prohibited structure.

He would also have to pay back his loan to his Solo 401(k) over a period of five years, so that might help him keep focused on reaching sustainability and profitability within a few years. What's more, when the business did become profitable, Chris could contribute up to $49,000 tax-deductible dollars each year to his Solo 401(k). He could also hire his wife to work for the business and she, too, could contribute $49,000 per year into her account within the Solo 401(k) plan. This would enable Chris to use his business success to fund his passive investment endeavors in an extremely tax-favorable manner, and progress more rapidly toward his wealth-building goals.

CASE STUDY:
Regular Angel

Benjamin Mathers was a 36-year-old freelance graphic designer who set up a Solo 401(k) plan. He did pretty well for himself, earning six figures per year and contributing at least $30,000 per year to his Solo 401(k). Between three years of these contributions and a rollover from an old 401(k) plan, Benjamin amassed about $180,000 in his Solo 401(k).

Throughout the course of working on graphic design projects, Benjamin came to know and mingle with a host of other entrepreneurs, including several specializing in web design, search engine optimization (SEO), and online software solutions. He saw this as an opportunity, and listened closely to his entrepreneur friends. The light bulb in his head lit up during a lunch with John Gilbert, an SEO specialist.

John had been working tirelessly for years to stay on top of SEO, the practice of optimizing web sites to increase their rankings on search engine results for relevant keywords. For instance, a flower shop owner in Seattle might hire an SEO specialist to get her Web site to show up on the first page of a Google search for the keyword "Seattle flowers." One of John's integral tasks was to stay on top of Google's methods for ranking search results. Google is constantly updating its formulas and algorithms, and most competing search engines follow its lead. After a few years of hard work, John found himself quite proficient at getting incredible SEO results.

During lunch, John mentioned to Benjamin that he was finding himself in a "catch 22." He had maxed out the amount of SEO work he could do by himself and couldn't make any more money until he hired two or three employees; yet he couldn't afford to pay new employees until he was making more money. A recent divorce had tarnished his credit, so a bank loan was out of the question. John didn't like the idea of adding the expense of a debt payment to his budget anyway, because he wasn't sure how long it would take the new employees to generate increased income.

Bingo! Benjamin liked what he was hearing. Because he knew John was a very talented SEO specialist, he asked, "What if I lent you the money from my 401(k)?"

"How can you do that?" asked John.

"Well, we would sign a contract, and I would just write a check to your business out of my 401(k) account," Benjamin explained.

"Let me think about it. I don't know if I want to go into debt."

Benjamin had some thinking to do as well. He always liked to find solutions to problems, and John's problem of not wanting to borrow money was no exception. He thought of something he had bookmarked several months earlier on his computer.

Once he got home, he found the bookmark: *royalty financing* or *revenue participation*. In this type of arrangement, the investor doesn't buy ownership in the entrepreneur's business. Instead, the investor buys *revenue* or *royalties*, usually a percentage of the business's gross income. Investors like it because they don't have to buy stock and cross their fingers in hopes of an "exit strategy," which usually takes the form of the company going public or being sold. Entrepreneurs like it because they don't have to sell part of their company or bear a fixed debt expense. Once Benjamin captured John's interest, they sat down to look at the basic numbers.

John's current monthly cash flow:

Sales Revenue	$10,000
Expenses	$1,000
Net	$9,000

John worked from home, so his expenses were very low. Benjamin pointed out how much money it would cost to hire employees, lease an office, and buy or lease furniture, a phone system, etc. John realized that most of those expenses would be unnecessary if he hired independent contractors who worked from their own homes on a project basis instead of hiring full-time employees.

John laid out a simple plan:

1. He would hire three independent contractors to work for him from their own homes.
2. The contractors' first tasks would be to improve the search engine rankings and traffic for John's own business Web site.
3. As more business came in from the increased traffic on his business Web site, John would delegate

much of the workload to the new contractors, which would allow him to handle a larger amount of total business.

John made some conservative projections and concluded that his business would be operating as follows after six months:

Sales Revenue	$25,000
Expenses	$7,000
Net	$18,000

After searching a few Web sites (including guru.com, sologig.com, and elance.com), John estimated he would have no problem paying contractors $15 per hour to work about 30 hours per week for him. He didn't need extremely talented SEO experts—he already had the system and only needed contractors who were proficient in general Web use and basic HTML (the simple computer language that most sites are written in). He estimated that he'd increase his expenses from $1,000 to about $7,000 in order to pay each of the three contractors $2,000 per month. From that point, his business would have the benefit of four people behind it instead of one. John expected he'd handle 2.5 times as much business, because he figured each of the contractors would not be as productive as he was. Plus, he would need to divert some of his time away from SEO tasks to manage his contractors. All things considered, he estimated his sales would increase from $10,000 to $25,000.

John figured he'd need about four months to reach this level of increased sales and productivity. This meant he'd need reserves to pay the extra $6,000 per month the contractors would cost. This was a perfect opportunity for Benajmin and his Solo 401(k). Benjamin proposed to put up $20,000 to purchase $30,000 of John's business revenue, payable monthly as 15 percent of gross revenue.

In other words, Benjamin would pay $20,000 to John's business and would receive, in exchange, 15 percent of John's monthly gross revenue until the payments totaled $30,000. If all went as planned, John would receive $10,000 profit on a $20,000 investment, or a return of 50 percent. His annualized ROI would depend on how long it took to receive the $30,000 of payments.

What was Benjamin's risk? If John's business didn't grow at all, Benjamin would have to wait 20 months to receive his 50 percent return.

$10,000 sales X 15% royalty X 20 months = $30,000

That's not bad at all. The worst risk was if John reneged and didn't honor the contract. Benjamin was comfortable enough with John to believe a breach of contract would be unlikely. Benjamin also knew that John was living on only about $3,500 a month, so even if the business didn't grow, John would still be able to afford to pay 15 percent of his already established level of income to Benjamin's Solo 401(k).

A 50 percent return in less than 20 months would be fantastic for Benjamin. In John's case, he was happy to pay such a return because:

- He didn't have to fill out paperwork for a bank loan.
- He didn't have to have a good credit score.
- He didn't have to bear a fixed debt payment. If he had a slow month with lower sales, his "royalty" payment would also be low. During a great month with higher sales, the royalty payment would also be higher.
- He didn't have to sell a portion of his company. The increased revenue would be *all his* once he had completed his royalty payments.

Both parties were happy to agree to the proposed terms, Benjamin prepared a contract in plain English,[28] they both signed the contract, and Benjamin wrote John a $20,000 check out of his Solo 401(k). It turned out that John's business grew even faster than planned, and Benjamin's 401(k) received $30,000 in payments in less than seven months.

In such a short period of time, the effect of inflation will normally be insignificant.[29]

---

[28] For sample contracts, visit FiveStepsToFreedomBook.com

[29] To combat inflation, consider drafting the contract to require repayment in gold. This is known as a "gold clause." Such clauses were made unenforceable by the Gold Reserve Act of 1934, but Congress reinstated gold clause enforceability for contracts issued after October 1977. Legal reference: 31 U.S.C. § 5118(d)(2).

Securities Laws

With laws, regulations, and the size of government increasing, we are entering a realm where bureaucracy and red tape stands in the way of conducting even basic business activities. Securities laws are no exception.

The United States Constitution gives the federal government a limited list of duties and authority and reserves all other rights to the states. In Article I, Section 10 the Constitution says, "No state shall... pass any bill... or law impairing the obligation of contracts." To clarify when and where the rules in the Constitution have to be followed, Article VI says, "This Constitution... shall be the supreme law of the land; and the judges in every state shall be bound thereby..."

Yet there are over 100,000 pages of federal laws and regulations while the "supreme law of the land" is six pages long. As it turns out, the biggest lawbreaker in the United States is the government.

Securities laws are a perfect example of this. It was forgotten that there shall be "no law impairing the obligation of contracts" when the Securities Act of 1933 was passed. Many of the most harmful laws are passed when we are emotionally distraught (consider the Patriot Act), and the Securities Act was passed during the Great Depression. This law says that a "security" (any document or contract involved in an investment) must be registered with the Securities and Exchange Commission (SEC). Today, this registration process normally costs more than $1 million in fees. Now, does that sound like a law that impairs the obligation of contracts?

What happens when the government goes after unregistered securities? In most investment transactions, there is an investor and an entrepreneur. The government calls the entrepreneur the "issuer." Normally an investment contract would state that the investor understands that the contract involves risk and he might lose some or all of his money. Sometimes, when investment money is actually lost, the investor complains to the government. In the case of an unregistered security, the government will often order the issuer to refund the investment money to the investor, which is a difficult task when the money has already been lost. The government may even imprison the issuer. That certainly seems to impair the obligations of the contract even more. The contract says the investor is to invest at the risk of losing his money, but the 1933 law allows the investor to sidestep his contractual risks, and instead ask the government to give the investor some of the entrepreneur's money or even imprison the entrepreneur.

How have entrepreneurs reacted to these law-breaking laws? Mostly by pursuing registration exemptions. Instead of paying $1 million in fees to register a security, an entrepreneur can pay about $25,000 in attorney's fees to prepare Regulation D (Reg D) disclosure documents in order to notify the government that a particular private security is exempt from registration. While Reg D securities offerings may be exempt from registration, they are not exempt from unconstitutional securities laws that impair the obligations of contracts.

Under a Reg D offering, the entrepreneur cannot publicly promote his investment opportunity. Instead, he is forced to offer the opportunity to only his existing contacts. If he pays an attorney $25,000 to prepare Reg D documents and then meets an investor who wants to invest, he cannot offer the opportunity to that investor.

The government has gone even further by classifying investors as "accredited" and "non-accredited." The former are investors who have a net worth of at least $1 million or an income of at least $200,000 per year. Everyone else is non-accredited. If an entrepreneur jumps through the hoops and forks over tens of thousands of dollars to do a Reg D offering and offers it to non-accredited investors, he still runs a huge risk created by unconstitutional government activities: if the non-accredited investor sues the entrepreneur, courts usually rule in favor of the non-accredited investor. The courts take the position that anyone who isn't worth at least $1 million or making at least $200,000 per year should not have to bear the consequences of a bad investment...unless it's a publicly registered security, of course.

Ultimately, any entrepreneur who is offering Reg D investment opportunities will generally exclude non-accredited investors. The law has told entrepreneurs to either register their securities on Wall Street or offer them privately only to people who they know that are already relatively rich.

Where do royalty contracts and revenue participation agreements fall in this whole mess? To the SEC, debt instruments are generally not securities. For one party to issue a loan to another does not create a security. This is because it is a simple repayment contract rather than a claim to a share of profits. The borrowing entrepreneur is not letting the investor share his profit; instead, the investor is getting his own profit that is independent of the entrepreneur's.

My conversations with SEC attorneys have resulted in complete agreement: debt itself is generally not a security. When I asked, "If you said 'generally' then what is the exception?" SEC attorneys replied that a security is created when warrants, or options to buy stock, are attached to the debt instrument because the stocks are securities themselves.

Royalty contracts share similarities with debt. In a royalty contract, the investor is not paid a portion of the entrepreneur's profit. The payment to the investor is an expense to the entrepreneur, as it is with debt. So debt is not a security, you say. That's right, but don't go too far down this path. If you develop a way to offer debt-like opportunities to lots of investors, Wall Street may not appreciate the competition for investment products, and it may ask its friends at the SEC to interfere with your business and impair your contracts.

That's what happened with prosper.com, lendingclub.com, and loanio.com. All of those services grew large enough for the SEC to ignore its own position that debts aren't securities. The lesson? If investors and entrepreneurs are going to come together to enter into contracts that aren't securities, it should be in a decentralized manner. If an intermediary broker makes money by facilitating the process, that broker will probably be shut down (by the SEC) if his operation becomes successful and grows. My solution to this problem is to simply remove the broker. If entrepreneurs and investors are using simple networking tools to share opportunities directly with each other, there is no clearinghouse or broker between them.

For example, prosper.com had over 800,000 users. Let's assume that half were investors and half entrepreneurs.[30] There were over 29,000 outstanding loans on prosper.com. Because all of them were packaged and serviced by prosper.com, the SEC had a single point to attack. If prosper.com were a meeting place instead, and if entrepreneurs and investors transacted directly, using free tools (and no services were provided by any intermediary), it is doubtful that the SEC would have shut it down. In fact, if the SEC wanted to assert its incorrect opinion that all of these entrepreneurs violated the law, it would have 29,000 small fries to pursue. Such a pursuit would be administratively infeasible.

Benjamin would typically be called an "angel investor," except the angel role is traditionally reserved for the affluent. Benjamin joined the ranks of *regular angels*—ordinary

---

[30] This assumption is for illustration. Many of the borrowers on prosper.com were actually borrowing for personal purposes.

people funding small business growth. Still, something else interesting happened. Once John's income doubled, he needed to reduce his taxable income. So he, too, set up a Solo 401(k) and started making tens of thousands of dollars of tax-deductible contributions to it. That put him in a position to make small and private investments just like the one Benjamin had made! In fact, Benjamin and John went on to make several profitable investments into other small businesses.

Angel investors fill a need not covered by venture capital firms (VCs). Whereas VCs invest several million dollars into a company and own a significant portion of the company (sometimes even hijacking control of the company in order to turn it public or sell it to a competitor), angel investors, who invest much smaller amounts of money, can be less hostile than VCs.

What's more, traditional methods of operating a business are being replaced by more efficient methods that produce more from less. This means that the next Google might not need $10 million in startup money—it might need $50,000 or less. And instead of being backed by a notoriously ruthless VC, it might be funded by you.

You needn't set off on a quest to fund the next Google per se. You can amass millions of dollars in your retirement account by helping small businesses get from *Point A* to *Point B*, even if *Point* B is well short of becoming a giant corporation. Think like Benjamin, and you will begin to see that you are surrounded by opportunities to make more money by investing in Davids than you ever made fooling around with Goliaths.

CASE STUDY:
Outsider Tactics

If you've read a complimentary airline magazine recently, you may have run across an advertisement for what some people call the "outside of the IRA" method. Richard, a 49-year-old software engineer, saw this advertisement and believed the strategy to be miraculous.

This method is promoted as a way to buy real estate with your IRA funds. Here's how it's presented.

- There are no IRA administration or custodial fees
- There are no restrictions on occupancy of the property
- There are no prohibited transactions rules
- There is no UBIT (Unrelated Business Income Tax)
- You can make personal use of a property purchased by your IRA funds
- You can use greater leverage with normal mortgage loans instead of low-LTV (Loan To Value) non-recourse mortgage loans
- You can combine personal funds with IRA funds without restriction
- You can practice self-dealing
- You can take depreciation deductions
- You can personally receive revenue and profit from the property[31]

---

[31] All of these restrictions are encountered with a basic self-directed IRA or 401(k).

To Richard, this all sounded like a fantastic way to do what would otherwise be considered an IRA prohibited transaction. So he called up the company that advertised this IRA "miracle." Instead of explaining on the phone exactly how this worked, one of the investment professionals crafted an engagement letter. The letter included thousands of dollars in fees that Richard would have to pay in order to take advantage of the company's program. Nevertheless, according to the advertisement, the company's product would allow Richard to use his IRA funds to buy property that he could leverage and make personal use of. Richard had $525,000 in his IRA and wanted to buy a beautiful home in Costa Rica that he had found online for $200,000.

After giving these numbers to the miracle-working company, Richard was told he was a prime candidate for its "outside of the IRA" method. So Richard paid thousands of dollars in fees to arrange for this miracle. The company sent him charts with confusing boxes and arrows. He took the contracts, charts, and paperwork to his CPA for a translation.

What the program was actually setting up was a series of "substantially equal periodic payments" (SEPP). In other words, he was simply distributing his IRA money to himself in a way that avoided the 10 percent early distribution penalties normally payable by anyone under age 59½.

The company explained that he needed to make a 20 percent down payment—in Richard's case $40,000. Because Richard had almost nothing outside of his IRA, he had to do a fully taxable initial distribution of $40,000 and pay a 10 percent penalty. As a taxpayer in the 25 percent tax bracket, he had to distribute $62,000 from his IRA in order have the $40,000 left after the taxes and penalty

With $40,000 in hand, Richard decided to make a down payment to obtain the property and a mortgage in his individual name. The company gave him papers to sign to document the SEPP schedule. According to this schedule, Richard would distribute $19,000 to himself each year, and this would then be used to pay for the mortgage payments. In order to avoid the 10 percent early distribution penalty on these subsequent distributions, he had to follow this distribution schedule until he reached age 59½.

He could make personal use of the property and ignore all of the other IRA rules because his IRA didn't buy the property. All he did was distribute his IRA to himself so *he* could buy the property. Richard closed the deal and bought the property after he took an inspection trip to Costa Rica.

Once he arrived back in the United States, Richard went to his CPA for further translation. He learned that this arrangement would directly cost him $69,200 in taxes[32]—or roughly 13 percent of his IRA value. His CPA gave him a multitude of reasons why this was the least tax-favorable path to invest in this property. The only thing the "outside of the IRA" method had done for him was enable him to make personal use of the property.

The miracle-working firm told Richard that the solution to his tax problems was the 1031 tax-deferred exchange. This

---

[32] The tax, including the 10 percent penalty, on his initial $62,000 distribution was $21,700. Each year $19,000 of additional distribution would create $4,750 in taxes. The latter distributions had to be made for at least 10 years. $21,700 + [$4,750 x 10] = $69,200.

would allow Richard to buy another property right after selling this one in order to defer the taxes. Unfortunately, the 1031 itself is often a major cause of further investment mistakes. With a 1031, when you sell a property, you have to buy another property within a few months. The new property must be more expensive in order to use up all of the proceeds from the sale of the last property. To eliminate taxation during the holding period of each property, you have to try to hit a "sweet spot" where you have enough mortgage leverage to create an interest expense large enough to reduce your taxable income without having such a high mortgage expense that it results in negative monthly cash flow. It's a silly game that completely distorts your investment objectives.

Furthermore, the 1031 confines you to a single type of asset. It is often called a "like-kind exchange", because the new asset must be the same kind of property. This puts additional restrictions on investment decisions, because the only "like-kind" of property you can exchange for foreign property is other foreign property. Richard can never sell his Costa Rican home to buy property in the United States through a 1031 exchange. Likewise, property in the United States cannot be exchanged for foreign property. Neither can other asset classes such as precious metals, private companies, and securities be involved in an exchange for Richard's property.

This causes several problems for investors. First, some types of investments may be better than others at certain times. For instance, if Richard decided he wanted to sell his property and get a position in gold, he couldn't use a 1031 to defer any capital gains taxes on the sale of the property. Rich-ard may come across an opportunity to buy stock in a terrific company at the ground floor, but he will not be able to sell his Costa Rican property with any tax deferment.

Even people who want to hold their wealth exclusively in real estate have problems. If their strategy is to seek out properties that produce high income relative to their pur-chase price, they must patiently seek a property that meets their criteria. After selling a property, 180 days may well be insufficient for finding such a replacement property. The strategy of selling high and buying low is nearly impossible to execute within 180 days. The 1031 exchange is useless for taking advantage of real estate market cycles, which may span many years. At one point of the cycle, properties are cheap, and at the other end they are expensive. Those who must do 1031 exchanges to satisfy their tax strategy may find they are either selling and buying at the top of the cycle or selling and buying at the bottom. Either way, the weak 1031 tax strategy and its restrictive limitations can cost investors more money than simply paying taxes on profits. In the case of retirement accounts, leaving the funds inside the retire-ment plan in the first place will ensure that taxes typically won't be due on the sale of plan-owned property.

From an investment perspective, there are even more reasons to avoid the "outside of the IRA" method. The entire benefit of a tax-deferred IRA or 401(k)—the whole reason why tax advisors have directed *trillions* of people's dollars into these retirement accounts—is sacrificed with the "out-side of the IRA" method. This important benefit is simple to understand when you look at compound returns. Paying taxes later means that money which would have gone to taxes is still yours for further investment. Paying taxes later also means that you have the government's money and are investing it for your own benefit. This compounding effect grows your account more rapidly. Tax-deferred strategies result in more wealth accumulation for the investor. This fact has given birth to an entire industry of retirement accounts and annuity and insurance products.

Inflation strengthens the utility of tax deferment even further. The government eventually wants its taxes. You can choose to pay them earlier or later. Remember, inflation is the process where the money supply increases and thus devalues the buying power of the money itself. In other words, the amount of dollars in existence increases dramatically each year, yet the amount of goods, services, and resources does not increase in the same proportion. Things cost more money as a result, and each dollar is less valuable over time.

Using tax-deferred accounts to pay your taxes later, means keeping the more valuable dollars for yourself. Later in life, when you pay your taxes out of these tax-deferred retirement accounts, you'll be paying with less valuable dollars. The "outside of the IRA" method caused Richard to pay his taxes sooner than he had originally planned. It also forced him into a situation where the future sale of his Costa Rican home would result in his:

A) Paying taxes on capital gains for the sale of the property, lowering the amount he can use to buy the next property and causing him to continue to pay capital gains taxes on the next property and the next and the next, etc; or

B) Using a 1031 as a short-term solution to a long-term tax problem. With the 1031, he will be restricted to staying within the same asset type and always buying within 180 days of selling. Ultimately, he will not have access to as many investment opportunities once he commits to 1031 exchanges.

Richard learned a tough lesson. He could have avoided the pain by doing further research before jumping into what seemed like a "miracle solution." Moral of the story: *investigate before you blow your hard-earned savings on something that sounds too good to be true.*

CASE STUDY:
Forced Appreciation

If your idea of forcing appreciation in real estate is rehabbing a "fixer upper," think again. Don't buy a house and pour money into it just so you can hope to make it sell for more. Hopes haven't been coming true for uneducated real estate gamblers lately.

This chapter will show you how to *know* that your property will increase in value. The first step toward believing this is possible (which is a prerequisite for actually doing it) is to understand how real estate is valued.

I first learned about forced appreciation through a seasoned real estate investor named Craig Harding. He invested in residential real estate for several years, only to eventually graduate into buying commercial properties—specifically apartment buildings. He made this transition because he realized that commercial real estate offers investors more lucrative rewards for their efforts, provided they get a little bit of education first.

In Craig's case, a few trips to the bookstore helped him realize how commercial property differs from residential. It all starts with valuation. Residential property, as you may know, is valued based on the *comparable sales* approach. A real estate appraiser will consider how much similar properties in the area nearby have sold for recently. Adjustments will be made for slight differences in the property, such as lot size, square footage, number of bedrooms, etc. A bit of math, based on standard appraisal practices, yields a value.

Appraised value is important in a real estate transaction. It is normal, particularly in residential real estate transactions, for property to be mortgaged, and mortgage lenders use appraised value to decide how much they are willing to lend on the property.

With the comparable sales approach, the value of the property is affected by what other people are paying for similar properties. The "crowd" isn't necessarily logical; values aren't always going to make sense, and they can swing violently. Even if crowds became logical, the fact that mortgage financing is required in most home purchases subjects housing prices to even more volatility. If mortgage rates go up, home prices go down. If insurance rates go up (think hurricanes in Florida), home prices go down. A buyer usually calculates what he can afford on his *mortgage payment* rather than his mortgage balance. Because the mortgage payment is PITI—principal, interest, taxes, and insurance—a buyer cannot afford just any total mortgage payment. If one item increases, another must decrease in order to keep the total mortgage payment within what the buyer can qualify for. Any increase in one item (interest, taxes, or insurance) will result in a decrease in the principal portion of the monthly payment on a new loan. Because the principal payments must pay the loan balance off in a set term (usually 30 years), lower principal payments must be tied to a lower loan amount and thus a lower purchase price.

$1000 Mortgage payment at 5% interest

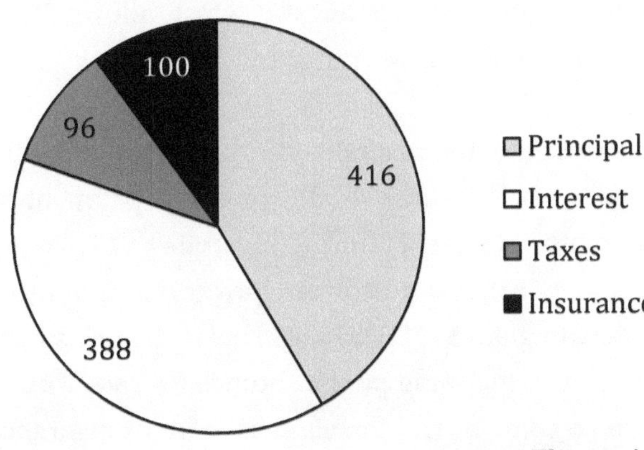

Figure 1

$1000 Mortgage payment at 6% interest

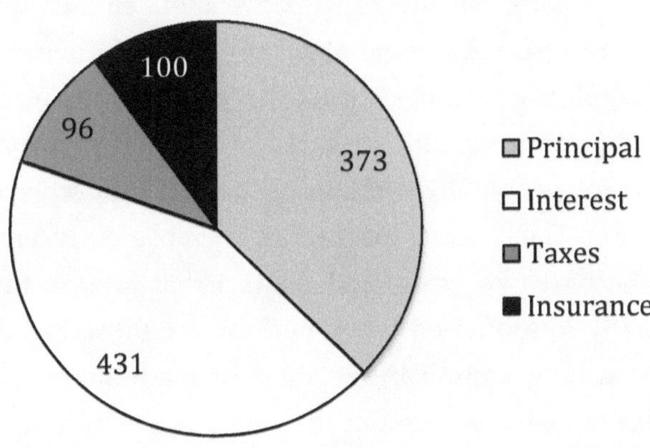

Figure 2

Examine the pie charts above. Assume a borrower can qualify for a $1000 total monthly mortgage payment—principal, interest, taxes, and insurance included. In Figure 1, that amounts to $388 in interest,[33] which allows $416 to go toward principal. These numbers accompany a loan of $150,000.

Now imagine interest rates go up to 6 percent. The same borrower with the same totally monthly payment will be paying more interest. Figure 2 illustrates $431 in interest, which allows $373 to go toward principal. This means the borrower can get a $134,305 loan. This is the same borrower, choosing from the same pool of homes for sale. Thus, home prices must come down. Increases in taxes or insurance rates would also force principal out of the mortgage payment pie and create downward pressure on home prices.

If mortgage loan approval guidelines become stricter (such as asking borrowers to prove their employment, income, and reserves), home prices are pushed down because the eligibility guidelines shrink the pool of people who are capable of purchasing homes. All of this spells uncontrollable risk for people investing in residential properties for appreciation. The housing market has been beaten and battered over the past two years, and the fact that interest rates are unusually low offers a bleak outlook for those banking on things turning around in the short or medium-term future. Interest rates have no room to go much lower, and current

---

[33] Because an amortization schedule has a different breakdown of principal and interest each month, here an average breakdown is provided.

interest rates are unusually low when compared with historical rates. Interest rates have nowhere to go but up, and this creates a probable downward force on prices in the future. The bottom line is you can't control the value of a house or condo, when the value is based mostly on outside forces.

How is commercial property different? Its value is normally determined by *income*. This is quite a convenient feature for those looking for confidence they can draw profit from properties. Craig's first commercial property was an office building that had several businesses renting office space. Before buying the property, Craig was able to examine the financial statements of its current owner, which showed him the income and expenses of the property as well as the NOI—(net operating income).

An appraiser divides that NOI by the local market's "cap rate" (capitalization rate). An easy way to understand the cap rate is to consider it the buyer's desired annualized return on investment if purchased free and clear with cash. For example, if a property has a NOI of $10,000 (per year), a 10 percent cap rate would mean the property is worth $100,000.

NOI ÷ Cap Rate = Value
$10,000 (NOI) ÷ 10% (Cap Rate) = $100,000 Property Value

In commercial real estate, the fluctuating factor is the cap rate. If a cap rate goes down, it means investors are paying more for properties. For instance, if the cap rate went down to 5 percent that same property that has a NOI of

$10,000 would then sell for $200,000. Commercial real estate buyers are actually buying income. If the local market demand for commercial real estate income goes up, the price of that income goes up (which means the cap rate and ROI goes down). While cap rates may fluctuate, their movements usually pale in comparison to residential price swings, because commercial real estate investors are a bit more logical than the hoards of insomniacs buying houses using a late-night "no money down" infomercial strategy.

After learning of some of the ways the commercial real estate game differs from residential, Craig decided to play. Not only did he see that investing for income was a solid approach, he also saw the opportunity to *force* appreciation. Appreciation is forced by identifying and purchasing a property whose income could be easily increased. In Craig's case, he looked for apartment buildings that were being managed poorly. He had a friend who was looking for a new apartment, and this gave him a convenient reason to inquire about the management of various apartment buildings in his town. He visited about 15 small apartment buildings for sale and knocked on tenants' doors to ask politely, "I'm helping a friend look for an apartment. How do you like living here?" Most tenants gladly supplied plenty of information about their experience.

Craig spent several days asking around and eventually he hit the jackpot. The tenants of one particular building shared an extraordinary number of complaints:

- The property manager was rude and unfriendly
- Things kept breaking and management was slow to complete repairs
- The people next door created too much noise late at night
- Most of the machines in the shared laundry facility didn't work
- The security entrance gate was stuck open and there had been recent burglaries

Sure enough, inquiring into rents told an equally encouraging story. Two very similar apartment buildings nearby had average rents of $800 per month, while the troubled property had rents of about $625. This was exciting to Craig, because the badly managed property brought in lower rents than the well-managed properties nearby. He found out that the owner was managing the property herself and had inherited it. His plan was to buy the apartment building and put a good property manager in place. This would enable him to raise the rents to the market levels. Let's take a look at the numbers.

$90,000	Gross annual income ($625 rent x 16 units x 75% occupied x 12 months)
($9,641)	Insurance premiums
($8,276)	Property taxes
($5,380)	Annual maintenance & repairs
($9,000)	Management fee (10% of rents)
$57,883	Net Operating Income

Craig also found that the similar properties nearby with average rents of $800 were also about 95 percent occupied.

So he made an offer on the apartment building based on the area cap rate:

$$\$57{,}883 \text{ NOI} \div 7\% \text{ Cap Rate} = \$826{,}900 \text{ value}$$

Craig decided to make this investment within his Solo 401(k). As the trustee[34] of the Solo 401(k), he was able to sign the contracts and checks himself. He offered $775,000, the seller counter-offered $850,000, and they agreed near the middle at $825,000. Craig had structured the contract in a way that gave him 30 days to inspect the property and the seller's financial documents. Within this 30-day "contingency period," he could cancel the contract if he wasn't satisfied with his findings. In this case, the seller's rent sheets, lease agreements, and expense reports matched up with the initial claims. Craig also paid a property inspector $3,000 to inspect the whole building. The property inspection reported findings of needed repairs, but nothing drastic or so expensive that Craig felt the need to renegotiate the contract.

Craig had about $800,000 in his Solo 401(k), but he didn't want to put it all into one property. So, he acquired a non-recourse mortgage loan to cover 60 percent of the purchase price.

---

[34] By its legal definition, a Solo 401(k) is a trust. While commercially marketed 401(k) solutions almost always involve naming a large financial institution to serve as trustee, naming yourself as trustee of your plan will give you the opportunity to avoid the fees, delays and restrictions that are common with financial institutions.

Here's a snapshot of the closing:

$825,000	Purchase Price
$14,728	Closing Costs
($495,000)	Non-recourse mortgage loan at 60% LTV
$344,728	Funds to close from Solo 401(k)

Take a look at his balance sheet...

Balance Sheet November 2005					
Assets	**USD**	**MPC**	**Liabilities**	**USD**	**MPC**
Apartment building	825,000	825.00	Mortgage loan	495,000	495.00
Other holdings	400,000	400.00			
Cash reserves	55,272	55.27			
Total Assets	1,280,272	1,280.27	Total Liabilities	495,000	495.00
Net Worth	785,272	785.27	*(MPC conversion rate: 1,000)*		

As the trustee of his Solo 401(k) plan, Craig wrote a check from his Solo 401(k) checking account to cover the funds to close. The property was titled in the name of **Craig Harding Solo 401k Trust**. That trust was also the borrower on the mortgage loan. Here's how Craig's debt service looked at the point of property acquisition:

$495,000   Loan amount

6.00%   Interest Rate

$2,475   Monthly Interest-Only Mortgage Payment

Debt service coverage ratio (DSCR):

$$\$57{,}883 \text{ NOI} + \$29{,}700 = 1.95 \text{ DSCR}$$

The non-recourse mortgage lender was happy to lend on this property. It had a Debt Service Coverage Ratio (DSCR) requirement of 1.00. DSCR is basically a number showing how well the property rents will pay for the property debt. It is calculated by dividing the NOI by the annual debt payment. Anything over 1.00 means there will be more than enough net operating income to cover the debt payments. A DSCR below 1.00 means the debt payments exceed the property's income. In Craig's case, the DSCR on his property was 1.95 ($59,883 ÷ $29,700), meaning that his NOI was 195 percent of his debt payments. This was good for the lender and great for Craig.

Once Craig owned the property through his Solo 401(k), he turned to increasing its income. The first thing he did was hire a property manager with a great reputation. Then he sought to address the problems he had uncovered during his initial research:

- He had the security gate repaired ($850). This helped to prevent burglaries.
- He performed the small repairs identified by the property inspection report ($2,836).
- He replaced the broken laundry machines so tenants could do their laundry on site again instead of traveling to a nearby third-party laundry facility ($4,342).
- He had the property manager deliver written noise complaint warnings to the two noisy tenants.

He also did a couple of additional things:

- He had the sidewalks, parking lot and building exterior pressure-washed ($375).
- He had the parking lot stripes repainted ($280).

The tenants immediately felt that they and the building were being managed with more care. What followed was the good stuff. The rents were raised. When new tenants signed a lease, it was for $775 instead of $625. As existing leases came up for renewal, they were increased to new rates of $775 – $800. It was difficult for existing tenants to complain, especially because if they went across the street to a similar apartment building, they would pay the market rent of $800. Some tenants moved to a less expensive area, while others were happy to renew their lease at the new rates.

Even better for Craig, his friendlier and more effective property manager was able to increase the occupancy rate from 75 percent to 87 percent. The average number of units rented at any point went from 12 to 14. It took only about 18 months for the higher rents and higher occupancy to be achieved.

Craig held the property for another year in order to solidify the record of higher rents and occupancy. Then he listed the property for sale. Let's take a look at the new income and value calculation:

$130,200	Gross annual income ($775 avg. rent x 16 units x 87.5% occupied x 12 months)
($9,641)	Insurance premiums
($8,276)	Property taxes
($5,380)	Annual maintenance & repairs
($13,020)	Management fee (10% of rents)
$94,063	Net Operating Income

Plug that NOI into the value equation with latest cap rate:

$94,063 NOI ÷ 7.15% Cap Rate = $1,315,566.43 Property Value

Here's what he has into the property

$344,728	Funds to close
$8,683	Initial repairs and improvements
$353,411	Cash invested

The income the property produced was as follows:

$36,038	Year 1 NOI less debt payments
$58,247	Year 2 NOI less debt payments
$32,181	Half of Year 3 NOI less debt payments

In the middle of year three, Craig was able to sell the property for $1,350,000.

$1,350,000	Sales Price
$81,000	Real Estate Agent Commission (6%)
$495,000	Mortgage loan payoff
$774,000	Net proceeds from sale

Craig had invested $353,411 in the property and received $774,000 as proceeds from the closing. Add in his profit from rental income during his 2.5 years of ownership:

$126,466	Profit from rental income (2.5 yrs)
$420,589	Gains (net proceeds from sale less cash invested)
$547,055	Total Profit
$353,411	Cash Invested
$547,055	Total Profit
154%	Total ROI (return on investment)
2.5	Investment Period (years)
45.37%	Annualized ROI

What a fantastic ROI! Best of all, Craig paid no income or capital gains taxes because this investment was held inside his Solo 401(k) plan.

By default, when a retirement account owns real estate through the use of mortgage financing, a special tax called Unrelated Business Income Tax (UBIT) is triggered.

Solo 401(k) plans, however, are exempt from this type of taxation. If Craig had used an IRA, he would have incurred the special tax.

Take a look at his balance sheet after he sold the apartment building...

Balance Sheet April 2008					
Assets	**USD**	**MPC**	**Liabilities**	**USD**	**MPC**
Other holdings[35]	512,000	379.26			
Cash reserves	46,589	34.51			
Proceeds from sale[36]	774,000	573.33			
Total Assets	1,332,589	987.10	Total Liabilities	0	0
Net Worth	1,332,589	987.10			
Previous Net Worth	785,272	785.27			
Net Worth Change	+547,317	+201.83	*(MPC conversion rate: 1,350)*		
Net Worth Change %	+69.70%	+25.70%			

---

[35] Craig had other holdings, some of which were in the stock market. While they appeared to grow measured in USD, they lost value in MPC.
[36] These are the newly-received proceeds from the sale of the apartment building.

Now, *this* is real estate investing. When this type of strategy is just waiting to be used to generate profits, why would anyone pursue any of the following strategies?

- Hoping that the real estate market as a whole goes up in value
- Trying to buy into "hot" markets that will appreciate
- Trying to find properties that need substantial repairs
- Trying to find distressed sellers of single-family homes who are willing to sell their properties to you for much less than you could sell it for[37]

Whenever someone says "I wouldn't invest in real estate right now because the real estate market is getting crushed," what that person really means is "I wouldn't *speculate* in real estate right now because real estate *prices* are getting crushed." Craig made an *investment*, whereas most people *speculate*. The difference is that investing requires a little bit of work and some reasoning.

Craig looked for apartment buildings for sale. He knocked on doors and talked to tenants. He selected a property inspector and later selected a property manager. He reviewed the rent rolls, leases, and bank statements provided by the seller to verify the property's income and expenses.

---

[37] If you buy a property for one price and resell it for the same price, there is no gain. Therefore, to create a gain you must buy the property for less than you can sell it for. The current seller should be able to sell it for what you can sell it for. Successfully buying from distressed sellers for a price lower than you could sell it for often requires manipulation and deception—not an advisable strategy.

He identified what would make the tenants happier and willing to pay rents that were in line with the market. That's real investing, and it isn't all that hard.

Anyone can use Craig's strategy. If you feel like you're in over your head, go to a local real estate investment club or meetup.com group and find seasoned investors to propose a partnership. Do all the work and let them check the math and documents and help you understand what they're looking for.

With all of the financial turmoil going on, there are plenty of mismanaged properties out there. Finding a multifamily property for which rental income can easily be increased opens the door to forced appreciation. At the time of writing, apartment buildings hold more promise than other types of commercial real estate. With companies going out of business and unemployment rising, office buildings and retail shopping centers are likely to experience declining occupancy rates and income. Apartment buildings tend to be less risky than office buildings, industrial warehouses, and retail shopping centers because everyone needs a place to live. Many other things will get eliminated from a personal or family budget before rent. Fancy coffee, luxury car payments, expensive clothing, eating out, happy hour drinks, and vacations all go long before housing. In fact, many people are already eliminating their mortgages by selling or abandoning their mortgaged homes and going back to renting apartments to save money. It's also a good idea to stick to affordable apartments.

What's the risk? Rental rates could come down, though probably less than the prices of mutual funds, stocks, or single-family homes. Cap rates could go up (meaning prices come down), but if that happens, it may make sense to hold on to the property. In Craig's case, holding onto his apartment building would still have yielded him an 18 percent annualized ROI.

It pays to venture into the understandable, logical, and somewhat *controllable* world of commercial real estate investing.

CASE STUDY:
Disqualified Person Partnering

Leonard Adler's story is part of the public record.[38] Adler already had a partnership that included family members. He wanted to create a new partnership with the same family members and invest his self-directed IRA in it.

Here's how the existing partnership roster looked…

Leonard Adler (himself)	6.5%
Steven Adler (son)	3.07%
Andrea Raskin (daughter)	1.35%
Jack Fetner (father-in-law)	3.94%
Fay Nadel (mother-in-law)	18.1%
Lois Zoldon (sister-in-law)	5.55%
IRA of Leonard Adler	39.38%

The issue here was *prohibited transactions*. Self-Directed IRAs have three main restrictions: No investment in life insurance, no collectibles, and no prohibited transactions. Complying with the former two is relatively easy, but the third rule is the subject of much confusion.

The rules describe two kinds of prohibited transaction. A retirement plan cannot transact with certain parties, including its accountholder, most of his or her family, or any-

---

[38] Adler/Janow DOL Advisory Opinion letter, July 2000

one who provides services to the retirement plan—all of whom are *disqualified persons*. I call this a "Category A" prohibited transaction. Second, a retirement plan accountholder cannot direct the plan to invest in any transaction other than one designed solely for the benefit of the plan. In other words, the accountholder cannot direct the plan in his or her own interest. I call this a "Category B" prohibited transaction.

As part of the 1978 Presidential Reorganization Act Number 4, the authority/obligation to govern *prohibited transactions* was shifted from the IRS to the Department of Labor (DOL). When you need clarification about prohibited transaction rules in real-life situations, you submit a written request to the DOL. Adler hired attorney Hugh Janow for this case. Let's take a closer look at Adler's situation.

First, *disqualified* family members are the accountholder's spouse, ancestors (parents, grandparents, and so forth), lineal descendents (children, grandchildren, and so forth), and any spouse of a lineal descendent (such as a son-in-law or daughter-in-law). The accountholder's father-in-law, mother-in-law, and siblings are not considered disqualified persons.

In Adler's case, the first three people in his partnership list (Leonard himself, Steven, and Andrea) are disqualified persons, while the latter three are not. Remember, a Category A prohibited transaction is one with a disqualified person. The question became whether the **investment partnership** in which the IRA will participate was a disqualified person **itself**. If a partnership is owned 50 percent or more by disqualified persons, it is a disqualified person itself. In Adler's case, disqualified persons owned only 10.92 percent of the partnership in total. The DOL explained in its Advisory Opinion (2000 – 10A) that Adler's investment of his IRA in this partnership would not violate the Category A prohibited transaction rule.

The next question is whether it was a Category B prohibited transaction—one in which Adler directed his plan to invest in his own interest. "In his own interest" meant an investment that benefited Adler *now*. Retirement accounts enjoy favorable tax treatment because the government gets its tax later when the accountholder distributes his account to himself during his retirement years. Naturally, the government wants Adler's account to be as large as possible by then. So, prior to his retirement years, the government wants his sole priority in directing his retirement account to be the profit and growth of the retirement account. Doing anything "in his own (current) interest" would divert his IRA plan funds away from profitable future investment transactions and thus escape future taxation.

Again, Adler wanted to invest his IRA in a new partnership that would include the same members as the old partnership. So, was Adler's investment of his IRA in this new partnership in his own interest? Let's further explore this.

According to Janow's letter to the DOL, the partnership would hire a professional asset manager. This manager required a minimum investment of $1 million. Adler's IRA did not have this much money. But doing a transaction that benefited the IRA was not prohibited. What mattered was whether the IRA's involvement benefited disqualified persons. Would excluding the IRA's investment have caused the remaining investors (who include some disqualified persons) to fail to meet the minimum investment requirement of the asset manager? If the answer was "no," DOL said in its letter it would not create a Category B prohibited transaction.

This particular Advisory Opinion has been problematic. With new marketers entering the field of self-directed IRA and 401(k) facilitation each month, the shortcuts some marketers take amount to very bad advice. Some of the longest-standing custodians, administrators, and facilitators have completely misinterpreted Adler's situation. The erroneous version of Adler's case goes like this...

"DOL says that it is legally allowable for a plan to co-invest with a disqualified person." End of explanation. It seems that many service providers in this field have ADD. They read the first couple of paragraphs of DOL's letter saying "it is not a Category A prohibited transaction." They completely ignore DOL's adamant warning that, in many cases, a plan co-investing with a disqualified person *is* a Category B prohibited transaction.

For example, let's assume you want to invest $100,000 of your IRA in real estate. You also have $100,000 of investable cash outside of your IRA. Those are the only two investable assets you have. After finding an investment property that requires $200,000 in cash, you consider co-investing your personal funds with your IRA funds. This is a Category B prohibited transaction because your decision to direct your IRA to co-invest with yourself benefits you *now*. It is in your own interest to include your IRA funds in order to give yourself access to invest in this particular property outside of your IRA.

Tweak one element in the example and it completely changes the legal standing. Assume instead that you personally have $500,000 of investable cash outside of your IRA. The proposed investment still requires $200,000 of cash. You could acquire the asset without including your IRA funds. The main reason for including your IRA funds for co-investment is to benefit your IRA. The government is fine with this, because it increases the value of the IRA, which increases future tax revenue when you distribute your IRA to yourself in your retirement years.

While both scenarios may increase your IRA's value, the first example involves a conflict of interest because you are interested in receiving profits before retirement, at the same time as you are separately interested in growing your IRA. Rather than measure and police the severity of conflicts of interest on a case-by-case basis, the government has chosen simply to prohibit them. This means the first example is prohibited because you have a conflict of interest, while the second example is not prohibited.

Some investors try to evade the prohibited transaction rules, but generally the Category B rules are impossible to evade. My opinion is that we live in a world of plentiful opportunities. Respecting the prohibited transaction law rules out less than 0.000000000001 percent of the investment opportunities that are out there. If something you want to do is a prohibited transaction, don't risk it; move on.

And now, a twist. If you actually go back and read the Adler/Janow DOL Advisory Opinion letter, you will encounter a curious little fact: The partnership's asset manager was Bernie Madoff. That's right, *the* Bernie Madoff—Ponzi engineer extraordinaire. Adler and the other investors in the partnership may have lost all of their money with Madoff, and this illustrates another critical point...

There are numerous ways to get undesirable investment results without breaking the law. Over the years, I've gained a reputation as an educator who knows the prohibited transaction rules inside and out. People come to my blog to ask me questions every week, often centered on prohibited transactions. I've been hired by banks, attorneys, and accountants to guide them and their clients through prohibited transaction analyses.

Adler went so far as to hire his attorney to get the government's blessing for his investment structure's legal compliance, yet ultimately he still fell into the trap of one the most well-known con artists in modern times. If I could go back in time, I would tell Adler to invest in real assets that he understands. Too many investors feel that their biggest self-directed IRA/401(k) investment risk is legal non-compliance. In reality, the biggest risk is making a bad investment, not non-compliance.

CASE STUDIES:
Small Is Lucrative

"Wrigley did it a nickel a pack and so did I," said Steve Barnett. It wasn't gum that made Barnett wealthy. Instead, it was one sweet deal after the next that gave him more confidence and encouragement to stick to investing in alternative assets, mostly notes. "I didn't have much money when I started. I had only $34,000 in my IRA." He turned that into a few million in a little more than two decades—one self-directed IRA transaction at a time.

All of us want to know the formula that creates a sufficient return on investment to produce financial freedom and wealth for a lifetime. Steve Barnett found that often-elusive formula. What Steve did, you can do too.

He's been crunching numbers for a long time. Now 67 years old, he hasn't stopped. Steve retired in 1989 with $34,000 in an IRA. In two decades, he completed over a hundred transactions that produced a whopping $2.6 million profit.

How did he do it? He used experience, knowledge, a constant hunger for financial education and a self-directed IRA. Let's explore some of his IRA transactions.

In some investment transactions, Steve created notes secured by real estate. At other times, he bought into a portion of an existing note. He loaned money to people and/or businesses that couldn't get funding from traditional sources such as banks. He took calculated risks and secured his investment deals, and he always understood his market conditions and the true anticipated profit.

STEVE CASE STUDY 1:
A Little Investment Money Goes a Long Way

In this next case, Steve bought a real estate note in second position and in just a few months was unexpectedly paid in full with a handsome profit.

"This little note was for $3,000 and I made $5,000 in just three months," he chuckled. "It was really weird that it happened that quickly." Here's how Steve did it. It was originally a 10-year note (120 months) at 6 percent. The balance was $8,850. Steve chuckled again as he thought about the $98.25 a month the deal put back into his IRA. But every little bit counts. And as you'll see, Steve's sound investment strategies have brought him sizeable wealth.

He purchased the note in second position on a home in Minnesota. The lien already had a history of seven months of on-time payments. The return appeared to be good, but what Steve actually gained in a mere 82 days was excellent.

Steve paid only $3,014 for the $8,850 note and the 113 months of payments remaining. Each month he collected $98.25. Once the transaction closed, he did an assignment on the note and recorded it to collateralize it and secure his position. This is important because it publicly records that the note has been transferred to Steve.

"This was a fun little deal—a great one," he reminisced. What made it particularly sweet is the fact that this note was paid in full early—extremely early. In just three months, when the note was paid off, it had a balance of $8,191.

The math looks like this. Steve invested $3,014 to purchase the note at a significant discount. He received three monthly payments for a total of $294.75, after which the borrower paid off the balance as part of a refinance. Steve's total profit was $5,471.75. "This is one of the very few second mortgages that I have ever purchased," said Steve.

Turning a quick profit with little risk

"It's unusual for my investment deals to go beyond four or five years," said Steve. In fact, most of his investment profits are captured within a couple of years.

It might seem that he simply waltzed into a fantastic investment deal, but that's not necessarily the case. There's always some level of risk in investing, but if you do your research as Steve did and understand the worst-case scenario, you will be prepared. In Case Study 2, the borrowers of the note were potentially nearing bankruptcy. Many people wouldn't touch this type of investment, but Steve identified his potential loss and saw a greater opportunity for high profit.

"The worst thing that could have happened to me is that I would have gotten all my money back," said Steve. While many people think that you can't purchase a note with a looming bankruptcy, Steve argues you can, and in fact, he did. "You can do anything you want to if you want to take the risk." Steve weighed his risk factors and decided to move forward. "The bankruptcy trustee could have effectively rescinded the entire transaction."[39] However, the chance for gain was worth the risk, "This was a very motivated seller who was anxious to get cash for the debt instrument before the judge discovered the asset."

[39] This would have undone his purchase of the note, in which case he would be refunded the money he bought the note with.

STEVE CASE STUDY 2:
Pooling Self-Directed IRA Money for Mutual Benefit

Sometimes, a single IRA account doesn't have enough financial power to buy into the best investment. That's when pooling IRA money can be very successful. In this case study, Steve and his friend William joined their IRA money to purchase a note from a bank at an extremely discounted price. They used a Certification of Participation Agreement (COPA) to define the specifics of the pooled IRA investment details.

"It was a fire sale of several loans," said Steve. Because of its poor lending practices and violations of state and federal banking laws, the bank offering the sale of the distressed debt instruments severely discounted the notes in an attempt to relieve the strain on its capital requirements and rectify its banking violations.

The bank offered to sell a loan with a balance of $49,000 and an interest rate of 10 percent for only $12,500—if the buyer of the note would close in three business days. Steve had to act quickly to grab this deal. He created a COPA and used money from William's self-directed IRA ($6,500) and his ($6,000) to complete this investment transaction.

They held the note for 15 months, collecting $489.21 monthly for a total of $7,338.15. Then they sold it to a private investor for $37,664.68.

"The real magic is possible when small amounts of money are united," said Steve. He adds, "This helps you control and reduce your risk in the debt-buying and distress business."

The table below summarizes this transaction.

Payments received	$7,338.15
Proceeds from sale of note	$37,664.68
Less cash invested	$12,500
Total profit	$32,502.83
William's IRA profit (52%)	$16,901.47
Steve's IRA profit (48%)	$15,601.36
Total ROI	260%
Annualized ROI	178%

Why a Certification
of Participation Agreement?

Steve uses a basic COPA that he has reduced over the years to a single page to help his IRA custodians comprehend his investment transaction details. "We attached a copy of the 'COPA' to the Direction of Investment Letter required by our IRA custodian before funding an investment." The COPA:

- Stipulates how expenses are handled
- Outlines liabilities connected with the investment
- Details buy-out provisions for co-investors
- Provides special repayment terms for investors
- Defines co-investors' stated terms, amounts, and conditions of investment
- Confirms parties are in agreement

STEVE CASE STUDY 3:
Alternative Hard Money
Loans Prove Profitable

Another profitable investment is a business loan made from your IRA. If you don't have enough funds, you may need to partner or pool IRAs to make the investment. Savvy investors know that unlimited investing requires unlimited creativity.

In this next case study, again using a COPA, Steve and a co-investor loaned $30,000 to a business in which the owners needed funds to write, publish, and market a book. The investment-to-value was about 30 percent, and the first-position loan was backed by a residence with 100 acres of trees valued at more than $100,000.

"You have to be careful about using a personal residence as collateral because foreclosure laws vary from state to state," recommends Steve.

Steve has counseled investors who failed to get sufficient collateral for their loans. "It's hard to imagine going through all the work of handling the transaction and then not getting collateral for it, but it can happen, and then it leaves you in a very vulnerable position."

Here's how the investment transaction worked. The co-investor put in 70 percent ($21,000) and Steve's IRA invested 30 percent ($9,000). It returned a healthy profit of $21,968.

The loan carried a 16.75 percent rate, was amortized over 15 years, had a monthly payment of $456.40, and had a 36-month balloon payment in the amount of $28,710.94.

Payments received	$15,974.00
Balloon payment	$28,710.94
Less cash invested	$30,000
Total profit	$14,684.94
Co-investor profit (70%)	$10,279.46
Steve's IRA profit (30%)	$4,405.48
Total ROI	48.95%
Annualized ROI	14.20%

These five transactions, along with over a hundred others, have grown Steve's IRAs to over $2.6 million in value. That's an average annualized return of 25.77 percent!

Balance Sheet 1987					
Assets	**USD**	**MPC**	**Liabilities**	**USD**	**MPC**
IRA value	34,000	34.00			
Total Assets	34,000	34.00	Total Liabilities	0	0.00
Net Worth	34,000	34.00	*(MPC conversion rate: 1,000)*		

Balance Sheet 2008					
Assets	**USD**	**MPC**	**Liabilities**	**USD**	**MPC**
IRA holdings	2,650,000	1,766.67			
Total Assets	2,650,000	1,766.67	Total Liabilities	0	0.00
Net Worth	2,650,000	1,766.67			
Previous Net Worth	34,000	34.00			
Net Worth Change	+2,616,000	+1732.67	*(MPC conversion rate: 1,500)*		
Net Worth Change %	+7,694%	+5,096%			

As measured in MPC, his annualized ROI thus far is 23.11 percent.

This is a great example of the way taking education and effort a couple of steps further can bring incredible profits. It can serve as a great starting point for someone with only a few thousand dollars. Even if Steve had started with only $10,000, a 25 percent ROI would still have built over $1,000,000 in 20 years. And this is with *zero further contributions* to his IRA. This is an incredible example of what can happen with a strong and consistent effort to find and execute lucrative investments over a long period of time. This shows you the possibilities. Now you can't say, "I don't have enough money to start with."

You might not be interested in working as hard and getting as high an average annualized ROI as Steve. But you might have more than $34,000 to start with, and you might be able to contribute new savings each year to your investment portfolio. For instance, if you start with $100,000, contribute $15,000 to your retirement plan each year, and average a 20 percent annualized ROI, you'll outdo Steve in only 15 years.

Another great benefit of small deals is increased diversification. If you have $250,000 to invest (instead of $34,000 like Steve), that isn't an automatic green light to make a $200,000 investment instead of a $10,000 deal. Small deals manage risk better because any one mistake or lick of bad luck is offset when they are many other investments in your total portfolio.

Let the possibilities sink in. If you want to multiply your holdings rapidly, you don't need lots of money to start with. Huge financial institutions can't systematize small and unique opportunities. These types of deals *do* require individual attention. That means doing small deals can carry higher returns. Steve did it (and continues to do it), and so can you.

Additional case studies from
Steve's deals can be found
in the bonus materials at
FiveStepsToFreedomBook.com

STEP 5: MENTION

CHAPTER TWELVE

LET THE UNLEARNING BEGIN

"Educate and inform the whole mass of the people... They are the only sure reliance for the preservation of our liberty."
-Thomas Jefferson

The first 4 steps, when followed, will lead you to your own personal freedom... one that isn't dependent on the orchestrated effort of other individuals. The 5th step—mention—is a matter of spreading the word about the importance of freedom and the simple plan to achieve it.

This 5th step serves two purposes. The first is to pay it forward. If you have had the privilege of having the path to your individual freedom pointed out to you, it only makes sense to shine the light on that same path for others.

The second purpose of spreading the word is a matter of believing in the larger freedom. This larger freedom was the founding principle of our country. Government promises to solve citizens' problems (and the oppression that comes

along with those efforts) is not new. History is full of societies that were not free. Our country was formed in the hope
of creating the first lasting society of free people.

It is abundantly clear that throughout history central
planning has been a failure. No matter how intelligent gov-
ernment-appointed czars are, no matter how much money
funds their programs, they can't know as much and act as
efficiently or productively as a free society in a free market.
Central planning just doesn't work. If it did, there would be
a historical example. And there's not. Instead, there are endless examples of the failure of central planning.

Much confusion comes from erroneously assuming
cause-effect relationships for coincidental events. We see
that our quality of life has massively improved over the last
100 years, the same period of time when the government has
grown massively. Along with that growth has come increased taxation and regulation. Today, mainstream thinking presumes that government growth, increased taxation,
and increased regulation were partly responsible for our
tremendous progress in virtually every area of our life. No
one ever asks *how* the growing government actually helped.

There's a mistake I've made several times in operating
my businesses. When I want to increase my sales revenue,
my first action is often spending money. I'll think of spending money as a business investment that will return higher
revenues. "If I write the check to pay for [insert any business
expense here], it will help to increase my business income," I
reason. The mere action of spending money on something
that *might* help gives me the feeling that I'm doing the right

thing. When I go back to examine it, more often than not I find the "investment" didn't really pay off at all.

This faulty logic is rampant within our society today. As taxpayers, we assume that paying taxes is patriotic because we are contributing our share of money to keep our wonderful system in place.

The truth is that our wonderful system isn't a matter of government programs at all. Government efforts aim to solve a problem. Yet remove the government program and people will, through organized or disorganized efforts, solve the problem and do a much better job of it than government.

I recently had a healthy argument with an employee of mine on this very topic. He said, "Some things the government just does better than the free market. Take the military for example." But a closer look will show the opposite. Even in our current war in the Middle East, there are legions of privately contracted troops and they wouldn't be there if the government troops could do as good a job. "Well, what about the development of the atomic bomb?" he retorted. I agreed that such a task usually costs a lot of money, which is best spread among multiple businesses and people. But all that means is there needs to be organization. What is it that makes us think organized efforts must happen through government monopoly?

Could we not have developed the atomic bomb without the government? If developing it was of utmost importance, are we really so stupid that we must have money forcefully taken from us in order to fund what's in our own interest?

There are many intelligent opinions about what the function of government should be. There are even intelligent arguments that assert there should be no government at all. While the term "anarchy" carries a connotation of chaos and madness on the streets, I've found there are incredibly bright people, respected and prestigious university professors included, who swear that anarchy is the best form of society. My point is that we can each form an intelligent opinion about how much the government should interfere in our lives and how much freedom we should have. But right now, I sense a growing movement of people who strongly believe we should have more individual freedom. Most just don't know what to do to head towards more freedom. Participating in the political process is a great start, but these 5 steps to freedom could have an even larger, quicker, and more direct impact if millions followed them.

A few years ago, getting millions to think independently enough to follow a path to freedom seemed naïve to me. But then Ron Paul came along. His perspective is powerfully honest and spot on. I've never met a person who understood Ron Paul's agenda and didn't support him.

Before I ever heard Ron Paul's message, I agreed with its principles, but was afraid to voice them myself. Before he gained serious attention in his 2008 presidential campaign, the topics of the ultimate harm caused (and lack of benefit created) by the Federal Reserve and the income tax just weren't on the table. It seemed as though bringing them up to others would make you look like a crazy conspiracy theorist. Then Ron Paul appeared out of nowhere (to many), loudly bringing to public debate what was previously whispered behind closed doors. The following that Ron Paul generated is a gigantic inspiration. There is a distinct possibility of increased freedom just around the corner. Not only is his "Audit The Fed" bill gaining huge support and many co-sponsors in the House of Representatives, he is re-igniting ideas that were dangerously close to fading away forever. Ron Paul was not elected president in 2008, but his campaign stoked the embers, without a doubt, and he continues to make way politically in the freedom movement.

Just as with political activism, taking the power back into our hands through *financial means* is an effort whose large-scale success requires word-of-mouth publicity. It's quite possible that the "Audit The Fed" bill could be disarmed in the political process despite a majority of informed people strongly supporting it. Our political process started out with a set of clear and simple rules (a six-page Constitution), and has mutated into a steamy, burgeoning pile of regulations and laws that even our lawmakers can't follow.[40] Sometimes our vote doesn't count, no matter how hard we try. I strongly hope the Audit The Fed bill is passed (without being stripped of its intent) by the time you read this. But if it's not, it is just one more instance when our votes, voices, and efforts didn't amount to enough.

There are votes, efforts, and bills surely worth standing up for. But I also believe there is *the* vote. In a free market, a myriad of individual financial transactions can vote for or against a private enterprise and determine its success or fail-

---

[40] When Timothy Geithner makes serious (but "honest") mistakes on his own personal tax return, and then goes on to run the department of government whose rules he violated, it makes for a ridiculous amount of irony and hypocrisy.

ure. I believe a public enterprise can be voted into success or failure as well.

There are two sides to every coin. We have been losing freedom by financial means. It is our choice[41] to continue holding dollars in our savings accounts and securities in our retirement accounts. The other side of the coin is regaining freedom through reversing the means by which we lost it. Just as a long, slow, steady information campaign has persuaded us to believe in certain illusions and adopt certain financial behaviors, a reverse information campaign can undo the shackles.

It is our choice to discontinue holding dollars in our savings accounts and securities in our retirement accounts. It is our choice to boldly vote "yes" for freedom through financial means. *The* vote can't be filibustered. Amendments can't be scribbled in the margins of our choice to *make* our freedom.

Whether it's for the well-being of those you care about or for the stirring idea of a free society, *mention* the path to freedom. Spread the word and support truth. The Internet-based tools we have today are incredibly powerful. Sharing videos, blogging, tweeting… the Internet truly is the great equalizer, and spreading truth has never been easier. While millions are tossing big media for direct, conversational information sharing, people are waiting for you to interrupt

---

[41] Most people are unconscious of the daily "vote" they cast in support of freedom-crushing institutions.

their conversations about Paris Hilton with something that matters. Do it.

We all want to be part of a team. People support Democrats or Republicans to belong to a team. Sports fans unite to cheer on *their* team. They'll even get into physical fights about it. The Super Bowl attracts record numbers of people.

This is a team for the history books. And there's so much more than a trophy or pennant to win. It's much easier to support freedom today than it used to be. Today your keyboard and mouse are more powerful weapons than the muskets and cannons used in the American Revolutionary War. There doesn't need to be blood. Wives don't need to lose their husbands and sons. Children don't need to lose their fathers. Widespread, sustainable freedom has never been so close. It's at our fingertips.

Here are a few simple starting points for spreading the word:

1. **Start a blog.** This is like becoming an expert web publisher without knowing any programming code or having any experience with web design. It's free and powerful. I use wordpress.com as my blogging platform, but there are also many others. You can use your blog to speak your mind, and you may be surprised how many people will listen. It's easy to start by creating short "posts" that link to other full-length articles that you find interesting. Cost: Free.

2. **Create a Facebook account.** If you haven't already, start an account on facebook.com. It will help you connect with other like minds, get access to valuable information instantly, and share information with your online network at the touch of a button. You can announce blog posts and events on Facebook. Cost: Free.

3. **Create a LinkedIn account.** This is another social network that is slightly different than Facebook but also has tens of millions of users. Cost: Free.

4. **Create a Twitter account.** Twitter has grown exponentially in a very short period. Only time will tell how Twitter will evolve, and we've only seen the tip of the iceberg. It is essentially a micro-blogging platform that allows you to publish very short messages, which can contain links. Cost: Free.

5. **Share videos.** Sometimes videos can deliver a message much more potently and vividly than text. Become familiar with sites like youtube.com and vimeo.com. You can share video you've watched by sending links to your contacts or publishing the video to your own web pages or blogs by using an "embed" code that is easy to copy and paste. Cost: Free.

6. **Meet up with others.** Visit meetup.com to find out about meetings on every imaginable topic taking place in your local area. There are over 150,000 meet-

ups each month. Most of them are either free or inexpensive. You can even organize your own event on their network for $19 per month.

7. **Connect with me.**
    Visit FiveStepsToFreedomBook.com to connect with me via blogs, Facebook, LinkedIn, and Twitter. This will also help connect you to other readers.

A Final Word

You're probably sitting alone somewhere with this book in your hands. I hope you're as excited and energized as I was when I wrote it. If so, take that energy to others. Talk to people in your daily life about freedom. Make new contacts online and offline.

This literary work isn't intended to be merely a stack of paper to adorn a bookshelf. It's meant to be a doorway into another world. In that world, we fulfill our human potential without interference. I assure you that world does exist, and there is no good reason for not going there.

APPENDIX

Additional Resources

FiveStepsToFreedomBook.com – Official web site for this book. Contains tools such as MPC balance sheets and cash flow statements, plus bonus materials.

GoldMoney.com – Precious metals dealer, storage facility, and transaction clearinghouse.

ShadowStats.com – Independent economic reports on the money supply, price inflation, unemployment, and gross domestic product.

CampaignForLiberty.com – Political activist organization endorsed by Ron Paul.

Mises.org – As the world center for the Austrian School of economics, the Ludwig von Mises Institute offers thousands of hours of audio and video as well as thousands of free books.

IRAAA.org – As the only trade association for self-directed investment professionals, the IRA Association of America is an alliance of specialist accountants, attorneys, custodians, financial planners, real estate brokers, and consultants.

Reason.tv – Home of *The Drew Carey Project* and other freedom-oriented videos.

JeffNabers.com – My Self-Directed IRA & Solo 401(k) blog that contains hundreds of posts aimed at demystifying self-directed investing.

Nabers.com – My unconventional financial planning firm. We pioneered the self-trustee Solo 401(k) that allows direct possession of holdings.

Recommended Reading

Economics in One Lesson
BY HENRY HAZLITT
This book does a fantastic job of tearing apart the faulty theories that make up some of our most popular beliefs about economics. Even if you're not interested in economics, you'll find this a brief and compelling read.

Crash Proof:
How to Profit From the Coming Economic Collapse
BY PETER SCHIFF
A hauntingly accurate prediction of how our housing bubble and credit bubble would pop. You can go to youtube.com to watch a montage of Peter Schiff issuing warnings and predictions on TV, only to be laughed at by reporters, anchors, and other experts. The details of his views are in this book.

The Collapse of the Dollar: Make a Fortune by
Investing in Gold & Other Hard Assets
BY JAMES TURK & JOHN RUBINO
James Turk is the CEO of GoldMoney and knows what he's talking about when it comes to monetary history and the impact of monetary policies on inflation and our economy. This was a great follow-up to John Rubino's earlier book, *How to Profit from the Coming Real Estate Bust: Money-Making Strategies for the End of the Housing Bubble.* If Rubino has one flaw, it's that he makes his precise predictions far in advance. His housing bubble book was published in 2003 and

his dollar collapse book in 2004. Read both and you may want to move across the street from him and invite him over for lemonade to pick his brain.

The Revolution:
A Manifesto
BY RON PAUL
If you truly listen to almost anything Ron Paul has ever said, the inevitable result will be a thirst for more. *The Revolution* is a great way to learn his message in a compact, to-the-point format.

The Creature from Jekyll Island:
A Second Look at the Federal Reserve
BY G. EDWARD GRIFFIN
This book pulls back the curtain to reveal the wizard that is the Federal Reserve more thoroughly than any other text. Enough said.

Meltdown:
A Free-Market Look at Why the Stock Market Collapsed,
the Economy Tanked, and Government Bailouts
Will Make Things Worse
BY THOMAS E. WOODS, JR.
For both economists and Joe the Plumber, Woods has compiled a well-documented review of what caused our economic meltdown and why artificial stimulus only worsens the pain.

Think and Grow Rich
BY NAPOLEON HILL

A timeless classic, this book is for everybody. Getting what you want out of life starts with monitoring and shaping your thoughts. Some call it the "secret" or the "power of positive thinking." Napoleon Hill does an astonishing job of teaching the reader how to follow in the footsteps of the world's most successful people.

Confessions of an Economic Hitman
BY JOHN PERKINS

If corruption and the rise of fascism are things you are skeptical about, read this first-person, autobiographical tale of a man who was on the inside of some remarkable swindles of gigantic proportions. Read this and you will know for sure that we owe it to ourselves to fight tyranny with individual empowerment.

Acknowledgements

Sincere gratitude is in order, as this book could not have been possible without the help of others. Bruce Pember was integral in collaboration and the organization of ideas. Tanya Herrera's assistance with research is greatly appreciated.

James Turk and John Rubino engaged in helpful conversations and graciously provided data. Dr. Alan, our editor, improved the manuscript by leaps and bounds. The book couldn't have come together in such a short time frame without the assistance of Anne Pollock. We're grateful for the collaboration and feedback from Joshua Geary and Jennifer Finke for many aspects of the book.

Debra Buchanan spent several years fostering an extreme thirst for scarce technical knowledge about self-directed IRAs. Legendary Gary tolerated and satisfied a seemingly endless string of questions and even made the process fun. We thank Terry White for diving in feet first to explore and develop the Solo 401(k) with us. Numerous blog readers helped mold the book title and cover with their feedback on jeffnabers.com.

Clients and friends who shared their experiences for the case studies are immensely appreciated. And a special thanks goes to Ron Paul for his relentless illumination of our country's most important topics.

The Complete Self-Directed IRA and Solo 401(k) Handbook

October Of 2009

I am often asked, "What is the best way to structure Self-Directed IRA & Solo 401(k) plans, entities, and transactions?" That is a loaded question as I have spent thousands of hours on full-time research and development of the answer to that very inquiry.

This follow-up book is written for those who have chosen to follow the *5 Steps To Freedom* plan and need detailed instructions for setting up and managing their retirement account as an optimized financial holdings vehicle.

Prohibited transactions, disqualified persons, UBTI Tax, Plan Asset rules, custodians, trustees, allowable coins, international holdings, LLC management, plan eligibility, maximum contributions, loan exemptions—it can get quite overwhelming and even when you think you've discovered the right answers, you may find various sources of conflicting claims.

Tax penalties for a faux pas can exceed 100 percent of the amount involved. Yet, I've found there are about a dozen fundamental mistakes that are common, yet easy to avoid. In *Unlimited Investing,* getting the rubber to meet the road in the most optimal (and safe) way is laid out in a crystal clear fashion that anyone can follow. This practical how-to guide puts the reader in position to confidently take advantage of the world's most powerful holdings vehicles. *Get it at UnlimitedInvesting.com.*

About the Authors

Jeff Nabers

As a nationally recognized educator, speaker, and consultant, Jeff focuses on the topic of unconventional personal finance. He is the founding member of IRA Association of America and CEO of Nabers Group, an unconventional financial planning firm.

Years ago, as a real estate investor and owner of a mortgage lending company, Nabers set out to learn the ins and outs of the self-directed IRA for real estate holdings. It turned out to be a larger endeavor than originally suspected. Nabers found himself traveling all over the country to pick up bits and pieces of useful information from dozens of sources. After compiling volumes of information in his mind, Jeff has turned to authoring as a means to organize the information to written volumes at the request of his clients and colleagues.

Jeff has served as an information source and/or writer for:

- Forbes Magazine
- Los Angeles Times
- Entrepreneur Magazine
- Realty Times
- Chicago Tribune
- Mint.com
- Various regional and trade publications

He's trained and consulted numerous attorneys, accountants, financial planners, real estate brokers, and investors. He's also been involved in thousands of alternative asset retirement account transactions. His firm, Nabers Group, pioneered the self-trustee Solo 401(k) plan, which allows direct physical possession of holdings.

Jeff's teachings are increasingly demanded by freedom-seeking individuals around the world.

Phoebe Chongchua

With a 20-year background in journalism, marketing, and customer service, Phoebe specializes in real estate writing. Her work is featured in: Donald Trump's book *The Best Real Estate Advice I Ever Received* as well as in *The Complete Idiots Guide to Buying Foreclosures*. She is the author of *No Worry! Five Steps to Peace Even in Chaos*.

Phoebe began her career in TV as an anchor and news reporter for ABC News in San Diego, California. She holds a real estate license in California and continues to write and educate consumers on real estate and financial issues in various columns and publications online and in print.

She is a columnist for *Realty Times, Bizymoms Expert on Real Estate*, and the publisher of *Live Fit Magazine*. After writing several articles on the topic of alternative financial strategies, she realized how little the average consumer understands the reality of where conventional methods lead us. Catalyzed to improve awareness, Phoebe's research dug deeper, and she continues to spread her helpful findings.

Nabers Group LLC

Jeff Nabers and Phoebe Chongchua work together through *Nabers Group* to help individuals find freedom through personal financial strategies.

An unconventional financial planning firm, *Nabers Group* is based on the virtue of capitalism with the strong belief that **better financial decisions are made when individuals make informed decisions for themselves.** Rather than ask clients to release their responsibilities, embracing independence is encouraged.

"Empowering individuals to better
themselves through financial means"

5 STEPS
TO FREEDOM

For bonus materials, tools, and discussion forums, visit

<u>FiveStepsToFreedomBook.com</u>